Firewall Services
Complete Self-Assessment Guide

CA00174982

The guidance in this Self-Assessment is base
practices and standards in business process
quality management. The guidance is also based on the professional
judgment of the individual collaborators listed in the Acknowledgments.

Notice of rights

Trademarks

Table of Contents

About The Art of Service

The Art of Service, Business Process Architects since 2000, is dedicated to helping stakeholders achieve excellence.

Defining, designing, creating, and implementing a process to solve a stakeholders challenge or meet an objective is the most valuable role… In EVERY group, company, organization and department.

Unless you're talking a one-time, single-use project, there should be a process. Whether that process is managed and implemented by humans, AI, or a combination of the two, it needs to be designed by someone with a complex enough perspective to ask the right questions.

Someone capable of asking the right questions and step back and say, 'What are we really trying to accomplish here? And is there a different way to look at it?'

With The Art of Service's Standard Requirements Self-Assessments, we empower people who can do just that — whether their title is marketer, entrepreneur, manager, salesperson, consultant, Business Process Manager, executive assistant, IT Manager, CIO etc... —they are the people who rule the future. They are people who watch the process as it happens, and ask the right questions to make the process work better.

Contact us when you need any support with this Self-Assessment and any help with templates, blue-prints and examples of standard documents you might need:

http://theartofservice.com
service@theartofservice.com

Included Resources - how to access

Included with your purchase of the book is the Firewall Services

Self-Assessment Spreadsheet Dashboard which contains all questions and Self-Assessment areas and auto-generates insights, graphs, and project RACI planning - all with examples to get you started right away.

How? Simply send an email to
access@theartofservice.com
with this books' title in the subject to get the Firewall Services Self Assessment Tool right away.

You will receive the following contents with New and Updated specific criteria:

- The latest quick edition of the book in PDF

- The latest complete edition of the book in PDF, which criteria correspond to the criteria in...

- The Self-Assessment Excel Dashboard, and...

- Example pre-filled Self-Assessment Excel Dashboard to get familiar with results generation

- In-depth specific Checklists covering the topic

- Project management checklists and templates to assist with implementation

INCLUDES LIFETIME SELF ASSESSMENT UPDATES

Every self assessment comes with Lifetime Updates and Lifetime Free Updated Books. Lifetime Updates is an industry-first feature which allows you to receive verified self assessment updates, ensuring you always have the most accurate information at your fingertips.

Get it now- you will be glad you did - do it now, before you forget.

Send an email to **access@theartofservice.com** with this books' title in the subject to get the Firewall Services Self Assessment Tool right away.

Purpose of this Self-Assessment

This Self-Assessment has been developed to improve understanding of the requirements and elements of Firewall Services, based on best practices and standards in business process architecture, design and quality management.

It is designed to allow for a rapid Self-Assessment to determine how closely existing management practices and procedures correspond to the elements of the Self-Assessment.

The criteria of requirements and elements of Firewall Services have been rephrased in the format of a Self-Assessment questionnaire, with a seven-criterion scoring system, as explained in this document.

In this format, even with limited background knowledge of Firewall Services, a manager can quickly review existing operations to determine how they measure up to the standards. This in turn can serve as the starting point of a 'gap analysis' to identify management tools or system elements that might usefully be implemented in the organization to help improve overall performance.

How to use the Self-Assessment

On the following pages are a series of questions to identify to what extent your Firewall Services initiative is complete in comparison to the requirements set in standards.

To facilitate answering the questions, there is a space in front of each question to enter a score on a scale of '1' to '5'.

1 Strongly Disagree

2 Disagree

3 Neutral

4 Agree

5 Strongly Agree

Read the question and rate it with the following in front of mind:

'In my belief, the answer to this question is clearly defined'.

There are two ways in which you can choose to interpret this statement;
1. how aware are you that the answer to the question is clearly defined
2. for more in-depth analysis you can choose to gather evidence and confirm the answer to the question. This obviously will take more time, most Self-Assessment users opt for the first way to interpret the question and dig deeper later on based on the outcome of the overall Self-Assessment.

A score of '1' would mean that the answer is not clear at all, where a '5' would mean the answer is crystal clear and defined. Leave emtpy when the question is not applicable or you don't want to answer it, you can skip it without affecting your score. Write your score in the space provided.

After you have responded to all the appropriate statements in each section, compute your average score for that section, using the formula provided, and round to the nearest tenth. Then transfer to the corresponding spoke in the Firewall Services Scorecard on the second next page of the Self-Assessment.

Your completed Firewall Services Scorecard will give you a clear presentation of which Firewall Services areas need attention.

Firewall Services
Scorecard Example

Example of how the finalized Scorecard can look like:

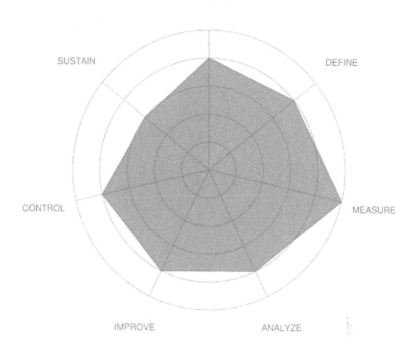

Firewall Services Scorecard

Your Scores:

BEGINNING OF THE SELF-ASSESSMENT:

CRITERION #1: RECOGNIZE

INTENT: Be aware of the need for change. Recognize that there is an unfavorable variation, problem or symptom.

In my belief, the answer to this question is clearly defined:

5 Strongly Agree

4 Agree

3 Neutral

2 Disagree

1 Strongly Disagree

1. What are the expected benefits of firewall services to the stakeholder?
<--- Score

2. Is the need for organizational change recognized?
<--- Score

3. How much are sponsors, customers, partners,

stakeholders involved in firewall services? In other words, what are the risks, if firewall services does not deliver successfully?

<--- Score

4. Which information does the firewall services business case need to include?

<--- Score

5. What are the timeframes required to resolve each of the issues/problems?

<--- Score

6. What needs to be done?

<--- Score

7. What are the stakeholder objectives to be achieved with firewall services?

<--- Score

8. Consider your own firewall services project, what types of organizational problems do you think might be causing or affecting your problem, based on the work done so far?

<--- Score

9. Who are your key stakeholders who need to sign off?

<--- Score

10. Whom do you really need or want to serve?

<--- Score

11. Are there any revenue recognition issues?

<--- Score

12. What is the smallest subset of the problem you can usefully solve?
<--- Score

13. Does your organization need more firewall services education?
<--- Score

14. Why is this needed?
<--- Score

15. What do employees need in the short term?
<--- Score

16. How do you identify subcontractor relationships?
<--- Score

17. What extra resources will you need?
<--- Score

18. Are there any specific expectations or concerns about the firewall services team, firewall services itself?
<--- Score

19. What prevents you from making the changes you know will make you a more effective firewall services leader?
<--- Score

20. Are there regulatory / compliance issues?
<--- Score

21. What do you need to start doing?
<--- Score

22. What activities does the governance board need to consider?
<--- Score

23. How do you take a forward-looking perspective in identifying firewall services research related to market response and models?
<--- Score

24. Who defines the rules in relation to any given issue?
<--- Score

25. To what extent does each concerned units management team recognize firewall services as an effective investment?
<--- Score

26. What is the problem or issue?
<--- Score

27. Did you miss any major firewall services issues?
<--- Score

28. Will new equipment/products be required to facilitate firewall services delivery, for example is new software needed?
<--- Score

29. What vendors make products that address the firewall services needs?
<--- Score

30. Do you need different information or graphics?
<--- Score

31. When a firewall services manager recognizes a problem, what options are available?
<--- Score

32. What situation(s) led to this firewall services Self Assessment?
<--- Score

33. How does it fit into your organizational needs and tasks?
<--- Score

34. What firewall services coordination do you need?
<--- Score

35. Are there firewall services problems defined?
<--- Score

36. Would you recognize a threat from the inside?
<--- Score

37. What is the recognized need?
<--- Score

38. What information do users need?
<--- Score

39. How do you assess your firewall services workforce capability and capacity needs, including skills, competencies, and staffing levels?
<--- Score

40. Are losses recognized in a timely manner?
<--- Score

41. How do you identify the kinds of information that

you will need?
<--- Score

42. Do you know what you need to know about firewall services?
<--- Score

43. Does firewall services create potential expectations in other areas that need to be recognized and considered?
<--- Score

44. How do you recognize an objection?
<--- Score

45. What are the minority interests and what amount of minority interests can be recognized?
<--- Score

46. Is the quality assurance team identified?
<--- Score

47. Think about the people you identified for your firewall services project and the project responsibilities you would assign to them, what kind of training do you think they would need to perform these responsibilities effectively?
<--- Score

48. Where is training needed?
<--- Score

49. Who needs to know?
<--- Score

50. What resources or support might you need?

<--- Score

51. How are the firewall services's objectives aligned to the group's overall stakeholder strategy?
<--- Score

52. What is the problem and/or vulnerability?
<--- Score

53. Do you need to avoid or amend any firewall services activities?
<--- Score

54. Will a response program recognize when a crisis occurs and provide some level of response?
<--- Score

55. What are the firewall services resources needed?
<--- Score

56. Are controls defined to recognize and contain problems?
<--- Score

57. Are you dealing with any of the same issues today as yesterday? What can you do about this?
<--- Score

58. Who should resolve the firewall services issues?
<--- Score

59. What is the extent or complexity of the firewall services problem?
<--- Score

60. What firewall services problem should be solved?
<--- Score

61. How do you recognize an firewall services objection?
<--- Score

62. Who needs to know about firewall services?
<--- Score

63. Who needs budgets?
<--- Score

64. Who needs what information?
<--- Score

65. Is it needed?
<--- Score

66. Who else hopes to benefit from it?
<--- Score

67. What is the firewall services problem definition? What do you need to resolve?
<--- Score

68. Why the need?
<--- Score

69. Have you identified your firewall services key performance indicators?
<--- Score

70. Can management personnel recognize the monetary benefit of firewall services?

<--- Score

71. What problems are you facing and how do you consider firewall services will circumvent those obstacles?
<--- Score

72. What firewall services events should you attend?
<--- Score

73. What are the clients issues and concerns?
<--- Score

74. What are your needs in relation to firewall services skills, labor, equipment, and markets?
<--- Score

75. What creative shifts do you need to take?
<--- Score

76. Where do you need to exercise leadership?
<--- Score

77. As a sponsor, customer or management, how important is it to meet goals, objectives?
<--- Score

78. How are you going to measure success?
<--- Score

79. Will it solve real problems?
<--- Score

80. Are employees recognized for desired behaviors?
<--- Score

81. How can auditing be a preventative security measure?
<--- Score

82. Is it clear when you think of the day ahead of you what activities and tasks you need to complete?
<--- Score

83. What needs to stay?
<--- Score

84. What does firewall services success mean to the stakeholders?
<--- Score

85. What firewall services capabilities do you need?
<--- Score

86. What training and capacity building actions are needed to implement proposed reforms?
<--- Score

87. How are training requirements identified?
<--- Score

88. Are employees recognized or rewarded for performance that demonstrates the highest levels of integrity?
<--- Score

89. Are your goals realistic? Do you need to redefine your problem? Perhaps the problem has changed or maybe you have reached your goal and need to set a new one?
<--- Score

90. Do you recognize firewall services achievements?
<--- Score

91. To what extent would your organization benefit from being recognized as a award recipient?
<--- Score

92. What would happen if firewall services weren't done?
<--- Score

93. Does the problem have ethical dimensions?
<--- Score

94. What tools and technologies are needed for a custom firewall services project?
<--- Score

95. Looking at each person individually – does every one have the qualities which are needed to work in this group?
<--- Score

96. Will firewall services deliverables need to be tested and, if so, by whom?
<--- Score

97. How many trainings, in total, are needed?
<--- Score

98. Are there recognized firewall services problems?
<--- Score

99. Are problem definition and motivation clearly

presented?
<--- Score

Add up total points for this section:
_ _ _ _ _ = Total points for this section

Divided by: _ _ _ _ _ _ (number of
statements answered) = _ _ _ _ _ _
Average score for this section

Transfer your score to the firewall
services Index at the beginning of the
Self-Assessment.

CRITERION #2: DEFINE:

INTENT: Formulate the stakeholder problem. Define the problem, needs and objectives.

In my belief, the answer to this question is clearly defined:

5 Strongly Agree

4 Agree

3 Neutral

2 Disagree

1 Strongly Disagree

1. How do you think the partners involved in firewall services would have defined success?
<--- Score

2. Who are the firewall services improvement team members, including Management Leads and Coaches?
<--- Score

3. Is it clearly defined in and to your organization what you do?

<--- Score

4. Has your scope been defined?

<--- Score

5. Is the team adequately staffed with the desired cross-functionality? If not, what additional resources are available to the team?

<--- Score

6. Is the work to date meeting requirements?

<--- Score

7. Has the firewall services work been fairly and/or equitably divided and delegated among team members who are qualified and capable to perform the work? Has everyone contributed?

<--- Score

8. The political context: who holds power?

<--- Score

9. What intelligence can you gather?

<--- Score

10. What are the compelling stakeholder reasons for embarking on firewall services?

<--- Score

11. How was the 'as is' process map developed, reviewed, verified and validated?

<--- Score

12. What sort of initial information to gather?

<--- Score

13. Where can you gather more information?
<--- Score

14. What would be the goal or target for a firewall services's improvement team?
<--- Score

15. What is out-of-scope initially?
<--- Score

16. How often are the team meetings?
<--- Score

17. Are there different segments of customers?
<--- Score

18. Is firewall services currently on schedule according to the plan?
<--- Score

19. Are required metrics defined, what are they?
<--- Score

20. Does the team have regular meetings?
<--- Score

21. In what way can you redefine the criteria of choice clients have in your category in your favor?
<--- Score

22. How do you manage changes in firewall services requirements?
<--- Score

23. How do you catch firewall services definition inconsistencies?

<--- Score

24. What are the firewall services tasks and definitions?

<--- Score

25. What gets examined?

<--- Score

26. What is the scope of firewall services?

<--- Score

27. How do you gather the stories?

<--- Score

28. What was the context?

<--- Score

29. When is the estimated completion date?

<--- Score

30. What is the worst case scenario?

<--- Score

31. What are the boundaries of the scope? What is in bounds and what is not? What is the start point? What is the stop point?

<--- Score

32. How and when will the baselines be defined?

<--- Score

33. What system do you use for gathering firewall services information?

<--- Score

34. What critical content must be communicated –
who, what, when, where, and how?
<--- Score

**35. What scope do you want your strategy to
cover?**
<--- Score

36. Has a high-level 'as is' process map been
completed, verified and validated?
<--- Score

37. How is the team tracking and documenting its
work?
<--- Score

38. Do the problem and goal statements meet the
SMART criteria (specific, measurable, attainable,
relevant, and time-bound)?
<--- Score

39. What constraints exist that might impact the
team?
<--- Score

**40. Is special firewall services user knowledge
required?**
<--- Score

**41. Is the firewall services scope complete and
appropriately sized?**
<--- Score

42. What key stakeholder process output measure(s)

does firewall services leverage and how?
<--- Score

43. Is there a completed SIPOC representation, describing the Suppliers, Inputs, Process, Outputs, and Customers?
<--- Score

44. How did the firewall services manager receive input to the development of a firewall services improvement plan and the estimated completion dates/times of each activity?
<--- Score

45. Has the improvement team collected the 'voice of the customer' (obtained feedback – qualitative and quantitative)?
<--- Score

46. Who defines (or who defined) the rules and roles?
<--- Score

47. Is there regularly 100% attendance at the team meetings? If not, have appointed substitutes attended to preserve cross-functionality and full representation?
<--- Score

48. What firewall services requirements should be gathered?
<--- Score

49. What are the dynamics of the communication plan?
<--- Score

50. What scope to assess?
<--- Score

51. Why are you doing firewall services and what is the scope?
<--- Score

52. Are task requirements clearly defined?
<--- Score

53. What knowledge or experience is required?
<--- Score

54. How have you defined all firewall services requirements first?
<--- Score

55. How do you build the right business case?
<--- Score

56. Is firewall services linked to key stakeholder goals and objectives?
<--- Score

57. Who approved the firewall services scope?
<--- Score

58. Have the customer needs been translated into specific, measurable requirements? How?
<--- Score

59. Is firewall services required?
<--- Score

60. Have all of the relationships been defined properly?

<--- Score

61. Have all basic functions of firewall services been defined?
<--- Score

62. Has a team charter been developed and communicated?
<--- Score

63. Is there a completed, verified, and validated high-level 'as is' (not 'should be' or 'could be') stakeholder process map?
<--- Score

64. What is the scope of the firewall services effort?
<--- Score

65. What baselines are required to be defined and managed?
<--- Score

66. Are roles and responsibilities formally defined?
<--- Score

67. What specifically is the problem? Where does it occur? When does it occur? What is its extent?
<--- Score

68. How will the firewall services team and the group measure complete success of firewall services?
<--- Score

69. What is the definition of success?
<--- Score

70. If substitutes have been appointed, have they been briefed on the firewall services goals and received regular communications as to the progress to date?
<--- Score

71. Do you all define firewall services in the same way?
<--- Score

72. Has anyone else (internal or external to the group) attempted to solve this problem or a similar one before? If so, what knowledge can be leveraged from these previous efforts?
<--- Score

73. What is out of scope?
<--- Score

74. Are audit criteria, scope, frequency and methods defined?
<--- Score

75. How do you manage scope?
<--- Score

76. Scope of sensitive information?
<--- Score

77. How will variation in the actual durations of each activity be dealt with to ensure that the expected firewall services results are met?
<--- Score

78. Are different versions of process maps needed to account for the different types of inputs?
<--- Score

79. What firewall services services do you require?
<--- Score

80. What is in scope?
<--- Score

81. What are the core elements of the firewall services business case?
<--- Score

82. Are all requirements met?
<--- Score

83. What defines best in class?
<--- Score

84. How do you gather firewall services requirements?
<--- Score

85. Are the firewall services requirements testable?
<--- Score

86. When are meeting minutes sent out? Who is on the distribution list?
<--- Score

87. Is data collected and displayed to better understand customer(s) critical needs and requirements.
<--- Score

88. What are the record-keeping requirements of firewall services activities?
<--- Score

89. How would you define the culture at your organization, how susceptible is it to firewall services changes?
<--- Score

90. What customer feedback methods were used to solicit their input?
<--- Score

91. Has/have the customer(s) been identified?
<--- Score

92. What is the context?
<--- Score

93. What is in the scope and what is not in scope?
<--- Score

94. Is there a clear firewall services case definition?
<--- Score

95. How do you manage unclear firewall services requirements?
<--- Score

96. Are there any constraints known that bear on the ability to perform firewall services work? How is the team addressing them?
<--- Score

97. Is the scope of firewall services defined?
<--- Score

98. How are consistent firewall services definitions important?
<--- Score

99. How do you gather requirements?
<--- Score

100. Who is gathering firewall services information?
<--- Score

101. Have specific policy objectives been defined?
<--- Score

102. What are the requirements for audit information?
<--- Score

103. What are the firewall services use cases?
<--- Score

104. Is there a firewall services management charter, including stakeholder case, problem and goal statements, scope, milestones, roles and responsibilities, communication plan?
<--- Score

105. What are the rough order estimates on cost savings/opportunities that firewall services brings?
<--- Score

106. Is there a critical path to deliver firewall services results?
<--- Score

107. Are approval levels defined for contracts and supplements to contracts?
<--- Score

108. Are accountability and ownership for firewall

services clearly defined?
<--- Score

109. Is the firewall services scope manageable?
<--- Score

110. What are (control) requirements for firewall services Information?
<--- Score

111. Is the current 'as is' process being followed? If not, what are the discrepancies?
<--- Score

112. What sources do you use to gather information for a firewall services study?
<--- Score

113. Will a firewall services production readiness review be required?
<--- Score

114. Has a firewall services requirement not been met?
<--- Score

115. What are the tasks and definitions?
<--- Score

116. Who is gathering information?
<--- Score

117. What is a worst-case scenario for losses?
<--- Score

118. When is/was the firewall services start date?

<--- Score

119. How can the value of firewall services be defined?
<--- Score

120. How would you define firewall services leadership?
<--- Score

121. Is there any additional firewall services definition of success?
<--- Score

122. What information do you gather?
<--- Score

123. How does the firewall services manager ensure against scope creep?
<--- Score

124. What information should you gather?
<--- Score

125. Has a project plan, Gantt chart, or similar been developed/completed?
<--- Score

126. Is the improvement team aware of the different versions of a process: what they think it is vs. what it actually is vs. what it should be vs. what it could be?
<--- Score

127. Do you have organizational privacy requirements?
<--- Score

128. Has everyone on the team, including the team leaders, been properly trained?
<--- Score

129. How do you keep key subject matter experts in the loop?
<--- Score

130. What are the Roles and Responsibilities for each team member and its leadership? Where is this documented?
<--- Score

131. Are resources adequate for the scope?
<--- Score

132. What happens if firewall services's scope changes?
<--- Score

133. Has the direction changed at all during the course of firewall services? If so, when did it change and why?
<--- Score

134. How do you hand over firewall services context?
<--- Score

Add up total points for this section:
_ _ _ _ _ = Total points for this section

Divided by: _ _ _ _ _ _ (number of statements answered) = _ _ _ _ _ _
Average score for this section

Transfer your score to the firewall
services Index at the beginning of the
Self-Assessment.

CRITERION #3: MEASURE:

INTENT: Gather the correct data. Measure the current performance and evolution of the situation.

In my belief, the answer to this question is clearly defined:

5 Strongly Agree

4 Agree

3 Neutral

2 Disagree

1 Strongly Disagree

1. What drives O&M cost?
<--- Score

2. Do you verify that corrective actions were taken?
<--- Score

3. How can you manage cost down?
<--- Score

4. What are the firewall services investment costs?
<--- Score

5. What does verifying compliance entail?
<--- Score

6. What would be a real cause for concern?
<--- Score

7. How can you reduce the costs of obtaining inputs?
<--- Score

8. How do you verify the firewall services requirements quality?
<--- Score

9. Why a firewall services focus?
<--- Score

10. Why do the measurements/indicators matter?
<--- Score

11. What causes extra work or rework?
<--- Score

12. How is progress measured?
<--- Score

13. Is there an opportunity to verify requirements?
<--- Score

14. When a disaster occurs, who gets priority?
<--- Score

15. What would it cost to replace your technology?

<--- Score

16. How can you measure the performance?
<--- Score

17. How will measures be used to manage and adapt?
<--- Score

18. What evidence is there and what is measured?
<--- Score

19. How do you aggregate measures across priorities?
<--- Score

20. Are indirect costs charged to the firewall services program?
<--- Score

21. How will costs be allocated?
<--- Score

22. Have design-to-cost goals been established?
<--- Score

23. How do you verify and validate the firewall services data?
<--- Score

24. How will you measure your firewall services effectiveness?
<--- Score

25. Was a business case (cost/benefit) developed?
<--- Score

26. How is the value delivered by firewall services being measured?
<--- Score

27. Are there competing firewall services priorities?
<--- Score

28. How do you verify your resources?
<--- Score

29. Are actual costs in line with budgeted costs?
<--- Score

30. Is the cost worth the firewall services effort ?
<--- Score

31. How do you verify performance?
<--- Score

32. How to cause the change?
<--- Score

33. What are your customers expectations and measures?
<--- Score

34. Have you included everything in your firewall services cost models?
<--- Score

35. What is the root cause(s) of the problem?
<--- Score

36. What harm might be caused?
<--- Score

37. How is performance measured?
<--- Score

38. How do your measurements capture actionable firewall services information for use in exceeding your customers expectations and securing your customers engagement?
<--- Score

39. What methods are feasible and acceptable to estimate the impact of reforms?
<--- Score

40. What details are required of the firewall services cost structure?
<--- Score

41. Have you made assumptions about the shape of the future, particularly its impact on your customers and competitors?
<--- Score

42. Do you have an issue in getting priority?
<--- Score

43. What could cause you to change course?
<--- Score

44. Are you able to realize any cost savings?
<--- Score

45. What is the cause of any firewall services gaps?
<--- Score

46. Do you have any cost firewall services limitation requirements?

<--- Score

47. Do you aggressively reward and promote the people who have the biggest impact on creating excellent firewall services services/products?
<--- Score

48. Are you aware of what could cause a problem?
<--- Score

49. What is your firewall services quality cost segregation study?
<--- Score

50. What causes mismanagement?
<--- Score

51. What are the firewall services key cost drivers?
<--- Score

52. How will effects be measured?
<--- Score

53. What tests verify requirements?
<--- Score

54. Where is the cost?
<--- Score

55. How can you reduce costs?
<--- Score

56. How do you quantify and qualify impacts?
<--- Score

57. Do the benefits outweigh the costs?

<--- Score

58. What causes investor action?
<--- Score

59. Where can you go to verify the info?
<--- Score

60. Has a cost center been established?
<--- Score

61. Are missed firewall services opportunities costing your organization money?
<--- Score

62. What do people want to verify?
<--- Score

63. How do you verify if firewall services is built right?
<--- Score

64. At what cost?
<--- Score

65. Are the firewall services benefits worth its costs?
<--- Score

66. How do you verify firewall services completeness and accuracy?
<--- Score

67. How do you verify and develop ideas and innovations?
<--- Score

68. What are the operational costs after firewall

services deployment?
<--- Score

69. What happens if cost savings do not materialize?
<--- Score

70. Why do you expend time and effort to implement measurement, for whom?
<--- Score

71. What are the estimated costs of proposed changes?
<--- Score

72. How frequently do you track firewall services measures?
<--- Score

73. What are your key firewall services organizational performance measures, including key short and longer-term financial measures?
<--- Score

74. What does your operating model cost?
<--- Score

75. How will success or failure be measured?
<--- Score

76. How are measurements made?
<--- Score

77. How do you measure success?
<--- Score

78. How will you measure success?
<--- Score

79. Did you tackle the cause or the symptom?
<--- Score

80. What are the uncertainties surrounding estimates of impact?
<--- Score

81. Who should receive measurement reports?
<--- Score

82. What disadvantage does this cause for the user?
<--- Score

83. What are hidden firewall services quality costs?
<--- Score

84. Are you taking your company in the direction of better and revenue or cheaper and cost?
<--- Score

85. What causes innovation to fail or succeed in your organization?
<--- Score

86. What do you measure and why?
<--- Score

87. What does losing customers cost your organization?
<--- Score

88. Are there any easy-to-implement alternatives to firewall services? Sometimes other solutions are

available that do not require the cost implications of a full-blown project?

<--- Score

89. How will your organization measure success?

<--- Score

90. Who pays the cost?

<--- Score

91. Are firewall services vulnerabilities categorized and prioritized?

<--- Score

92. What is measured? Why?

<--- Score

93. When are costs are incurred?

<--- Score

94. What are the types and number of measures to use?

<--- Score

95. Which measures and indicators matter?

<--- Score

96. Which firewall services impacts are significant?

<--- Score

97. What are the current costs of the firewall services process?

<--- Score

98. What are allowable costs?

<--- Score

99. What is the total fixed cost?
<--- Score

100. Among the firewall services product and service cost to be estimated, which is considered hardest to estimate?
<--- Score

101. How do you measure efficient delivery of firewall services services?
<--- Score

102. What are the costs of reform?
<--- Score

103. Are supply costs steady or fluctuating?
<--- Score

104. Are there measurements based on task performance?
<--- Score

105. How can a firewall services test verify your ideas or assumptions?
<--- Score

106. How do you verify the authenticity of the data and information used?
<--- Score

107. What users will be impacted?
<--- Score

108. How can you measure firewall services in a systematic way?

<--- Score

109. What are the costs?
<--- Score

110. What is an unallowable cost?
<--- Score

111. What is the cost of rework?
<--- Score

112. What is the firewall services business impact?
<--- Score

113. How are you verifying it?
<--- Score

114. Are the units of measure consistent?
<--- Score

115. How do you prevent mis-estimating cost?
<--- Score

116. Which costs should be taken into account?
<--- Score

117. Are the measurements objective?
<--- Score

118. What are you verifying?
<--- Score

119. Is the solution cost-effective?
<--- Score

120. How do you measure variability?

<--- Score

121. What are your operating costs?
<--- Score

122. Do you effectively measure and reward individual and team performance?
<--- Score

123. How frequently do you verify your firewall services strategy?
<--- Score

124. What can be used to verify compliance?
<--- Score

125. How are costs allocated?
<--- Score

126. Is it possible to estimate the impact of unanticipated complexity such as wrong or failed assumptions, feedback, etcetera on proposed reforms?
<--- Score

127. Does management have the right priorities among projects?
<--- Score

128. What measurements are possible, practicable and meaningful?
<--- Score

129. What does a Test Case verify?
<--- Score

130. What could cause delays in the schedule?
<--- Score

131. What potential environmental factors impact the firewall services effort?
<--- Score

132. How do you control the overall costs of your work processes?
<--- Score

133. Does a firewall services quantification method exist?
<--- Score

134. What are the costs and benefits?
<--- Score

Add up total points for this section:
_____ = Total points for this section

Divided by: _____ (number of statements answered) = _____
Average score for this section

Transfer your score to the firewall services Index at the beginning of the Self-Assessment.

CRITERION #4: ANALYZE:

INTENT: Analyze causes, assumptions
and hypotheses.

In my belief, the answer to this
question is clearly defined:

5 Strongly Agree

4 Agree

3 Neutral

2 Disagree

1 Strongly Disagree

1. What are your current levels and trends in key measures or indicators of firewall services product and process performance that are important to and directly serve your customers? How do these results compare with the performance of your competitors and other organizations with similar offerings?
<--- Score

2. Should you invest in industry-recognized qualifications?

<--- Score

3. What does the data say about the performance of the stakeholder process?
<--- Score

4. How do you ensure that the firewall services opportunity is realistic?
<--- Score

5. What are your best practices for minimizing firewall services project risk, while demonstrating incremental value and quick wins throughout the firewall services project lifecycle?
<--- Score

6. What tools were used to generate the list of possible causes?
<--- Score

7. What training and qualifications will you need?
<--- Score

8. Record-keeping requirements flow from the records needed as inputs, outputs, controls and for transformation of a firewall services process, are the records needed as inputs to the firewall services process available?
<--- Score

9. Do your contracts/agreements contain data security obligations?
<--- Score

10. How has the firewall services data been gathered?

<--- Score

11. Who gets your output?
<--- Score

12. How is the data gathered?
<--- Score

13. How does the organization define, manage, and improve its firewall services processes?
<--- Score

14. What other jobs or tasks affect the performance of the steps in the firewall services process?
<--- Score

15. What qualifies as competition?
<--- Score

16. What did the team gain from developing a sub-process map?
<--- Score

17. Do quality systems drive continuous improvement?
<--- Score

18. Who owns what data?
<--- Score

19. Think about the functions involved in your firewall services project, what processes flow from these functions?
<--- Score

20. Is the suppliers process defined and controlled?
<--- Score

21. How will the change process be managed?
<--- Score

22. What data is gathered?
<--- Score

23. Has an output goal been set?
<--- Score

24. Who is involved in the management review process?
<--- Score

25. What process improvements will be needed?
<--- Score

26. Was a detailed process map created to amplify critical steps of the 'as is' stakeholder process?
<--- Score

27. Have any additional benefits been identified that will result from closing all or most of the gaps?
<--- Score

28. How many input/output points does it require?
<--- Score

29. What methods do you use to gather firewall services data?
<--- Score

30. Were there any improvement opportunities identified from the process analysis?

<--- Score

31. What is the oversight process?
<--- Score

32. What are your current levels and trends in key firewall services measures or indicators of product and process performance that are important to and directly serve your customers?
<--- Score

33. Where is the data coming from to measure compliance?
<--- Score

34. Are firewall services changes recognized early enough to be approved through the regular process?
<--- Score

35. What output to create?
<--- Score

36. What is the output?
<--- Score

37. Is the performance gap determined?
<--- Score

38. What conclusions were drawn from the team's data collection and analysis? How did the team reach these conclusions?
<--- Score

39. What is the cost of poor quality as supported by the team's analysis?
<--- Score

40. Are your outputs consistent?
<--- Score

41. What are your firewall services processes?
<--- Score

42. Are all team members qualified for all tasks?
<--- Score

43. How was the detailed process map generated, verified, and validated?
<--- Score

44. Who will facilitate the team and process?
<--- Score

45. What kind of crime could a potential new hire have committed that would not only not disqualify him/her from being hired by your organization, but would actually indicate that he/she might be a particularly good fit?
<--- Score

46. What, related to, firewall services processes does your organization outsource?
<--- Score

47. How much data can be collected in the given timeframe?
<--- Score

48. Is data and process analysis, root cause analysis and quantifying the gap/opportunity in place?
<--- Score

49. What firewall services data should be managed?
<--- Score

50. Is the firewall services process severely broken such that a re-design is necessary?
<--- Score

51. What is your organizations system for selecting qualified vendors?
<--- Score

52. Were Pareto charts (or similar) used to portray the 'heavy hitters' (or key sources of variation)?
<--- Score

53. Is there a strict change management process?
<--- Score

54. What resources go in to get the desired output?
<--- Score

55. Think about some of the processes you undertake within your organization, which do you own?
<--- Score

56. What will drive firewall services change?
<--- Score

57. Is the final output clearly identified?
<--- Score

58. What qualifications do firewall services leaders need?
<--- Score

59. Is there any way to speed up the process?
<--- Score

60. What types of data do your firewall services indicators require?
<--- Score

61. What are the firewall services design outputs?
<--- Score

62. Has data output been validated?
<--- Score

63. What were the crucial 'moments of truth' on the process map?
<--- Score

64. How do mission and objectives affect the firewall services processes of your organization?
<--- Score

65. How do your work systems and key work processes relate to and capitalize on your core competencies?
<--- Score

66. How is the firewall services Value Stream Mapping managed?
<--- Score

67. Do staff qualifications match your project?
<--- Score

68. Who qualifies to gain access to data?
<--- Score

69. Do you, as a leader, bounce back quickly from setbacks?

<--- Score

70. Do several people in different organizational units assist with the firewall services process?

<--- Score

71. How are outputs preserved and protected?

<--- Score

72. What firewall services data should be collected?

<--- Score

73. What are the processes for audit reporting and management?

<--- Score

74. Who is involved with workflow mapping?

<--- Score

75. What are the revised rough estimates of the financial savings/opportunity for firewall services improvements?

<--- Score

76. How do you promote understanding that opportunity for improvement is not criticism of the status quo, or the people who created the status quo?

<--- Score

77. What is the firewall services Driver?

<--- Score

78. How will the firewall services data be captured?

<--- Score

79. How will the data be checked for quality?
<--- Score

80. Can you add value to the current firewall services decision-making process (largely qualitative) by incorporating uncertainty modeling (more quantitative)?
<--- Score

81. Where is firewall services data gathered?
<--- Score

82. Do your leaders quickly bounce back from setbacks?
<--- Score

83. Which firewall services data should be retained?
<--- Score

84. What other organizational variables, such as reward systems or communication systems, affect the performance of this firewall services process?
<--- Score

85. How do you implement and manage your work processes to ensure that they meet design requirements?
<--- Score

86. Have the problem and goal statements been updated to reflect the additional knowledge gained from the analyze phase?
<--- Score

87. How will corresponding data be collected?

<--- Score

88. How difficult is it to qualify what firewall services ROI is?

<--- Score

89. What process should you select for improvement?

<--- Score

90. Do you have the authority to produce the output?

<--- Score

91. What are your outputs?

<--- Score

92. What data do you need to collect?

<--- Score

93. Identify an operational issue in your organization, for example, could a particular task be done more quickly or more efficiently by firewall services?

<--- Score

94. What firewall services metrics are outputs of the process?

<--- Score

95. How do you identify specific firewall services investment opportunities and emerging trends?

<--- Score

96. An organizationally feasible system request is one that considers the mission, goals and objectives of the organization, key questions are: is the firewall services solution request practical and will it solve a problem

or take advantage of an opportunity to achieve company goals?

<--- Score

97. Who will gather what data?

<--- Score

98. What is the Value Stream Mapping?

<--- Score

99. What firewall services data will be collected?

<--- Score

100. How do you define collaboration and team output?

<--- Score

101. A compounding model resolution with available relevant data can often provide insight towards a solution methodology; which firewall services models, tools and techniques are necessary?

<--- Score

102. How can risk management be tied procedurally to process elements?

<--- Score

103. What are evaluation criteria for the output?

<--- Score

104. What qualifications and skills do you need?

<--- Score

105. What is the complexity of the output produced?

<--- Score

106. What internal processes need improvement?
<--- Score

107. What is your organizations process which leads to recognition of value generation?
<--- Score

108. Where can you get qualified talent today?
<--- Score

109. What qualifications are necessary?
<--- Score

110. Are you missing firewall services opportunities?
<--- Score

111. What quality tools were used to get through the analyze phase?
<--- Score

112. What systems/processes must you excel at?
<--- Score

113. How is data used for program management and improvement?
<--- Score

114. Is pre-qualification of suppliers carried out?
<--- Score

115. Were any designed experiments used to generate additional insight into the data analysis?
<--- Score

116. How is the way you as the leader think and

process information affecting your organizational culture?

<--- Score

117. What qualifications are needed?

<--- Score

118. What firewall services data do you gather or use now?

<--- Score

119. What are the best opportunities for value improvement?

<--- Score

120. When should a process be art not science?

<--- Score

121. What are the firewall services business drivers?

<--- Score

122. What were the financial benefits resulting from any 'ground fruit or low-hanging fruit' (quick fixes)?

<--- Score

123. Do you understand your management processes today?

<--- Score

124. What do you need to qualify?

<--- Score

125. What are the disruptive firewall services technologies that enable your organization to radically change your business processes?

<--- Score

126. What are the personnel training and qualifications required?
<--- Score

127. What information qualified as important?
<--- Score

128. Do your employees have the opportunity to do what they do best everyday?
<--- Score

129. What tools were used to narrow the list of possible causes?
<--- Score

130. How is firewall services data gathered?
<--- Score

131. Was a cause-and-effect diagram used to explore the different types of causes (or sources of variation)?
<--- Score

132. Is the gap/opportunity displayed and communicated in financial terms?
<--- Score

133. Is there an established change management process?
<--- Score

Add up total points for this section:
_ _ _ _ _ = Total points for this section

Divided by: _ _ _ _ _ _ (number of

statements answered) = _____
Average score for this section

Transfer your score to the firewall
services Index at the beginning of the
Self-Assessment.

CRITERION #5: IMPROVE:

1. How do you improve firewall services service perception, and satisfaction?
<--- Score

2. What criteria will you use to assess your firewall services risks?
<--- Score

3. Risk events: what are the things that could go

wrong?

<--- Score

4. For estimation problems, how do you develop an estimation statement?

<--- Score

5. What improvements have been achieved?

<--- Score

6. Who will be using the results of the measurement activities?

<--- Score

7. How do you mitigate firewall services risk?

<--- Score

8. Who are the people involved in developing and implementing firewall services?

<--- Score

9. Is the firewall services documentation thorough?

<--- Score

10. What are the concrete firewall services results?

<--- Score

11. Is the measure of success for firewall services understandable to a variety of people?

<--- Score

12. How is continuous improvement applied to risk management?

<--- Score

13. How do you measure progress and evaluate training effectiveness?
<--- Score

14. In the past few months, what is the smallest change you have made that has had the biggest positive result? What was it about that small change that produced the large return?
<--- Score

15. How do you improve your likelihood of success ?
<--- Score

16. Can you integrate quality management and risk management?
<--- Score

17. Do you need to do a usability evaluation?
<--- Score

18. Who do you report firewall services results to?
<--- Score

19. What is the firewall services's sustainability risk?
<--- Score

20. How can you better manage risk?
<--- Score

21. How can the phases of firewall services development be identified?
<--- Score

22. If you could go back in time five years, what decision would you make differently? What is your best guess as to what decision you're making today

you might regret five years from now?
<--- Score

23. Is the firewall services solution sustainable?
<--- Score

24. What is the magnitude of the improvements?
<--- Score

25. Do those selected for the firewall services team have a good general understanding of what firewall services is all about?
<--- Score

26. Are the key business and technology risks being managed?
<--- Score

27. Have you achieved firewall services improvements?
<--- Score

28. What tools were used to tap into the creativity and encourage 'outside the box' thinking?
<--- Score

29. How scalable is your firewall services solution?
<--- Score

30. What can you do to improve?
<--- Score

31. Are the risks fully understood, reasonable and manageable?
<--- Score

32. How do you improve productivity?
<--- Score

33. Will the controls trigger any other risks?
<--- Score

34. How significant is the improvement in the eyes of the end user?
<--- Score

35. How can skill-level changes improve firewall services?
<--- Score

36. How will you measure the results?
<--- Score

37. Is risk periodically assessed?
<--- Score

38. What tools were most useful during the improve phase?
<--- Score

39. What needs improvement? Why?
<--- Score

40. Do vendor agreements bring new compliance risk ?
<--- Score

41. Can you identify any significant risks or exposures to firewall services third- parties (vendors, service providers, alliance partners etc) that concern you?
<--- Score

42. What resources are required for the improvement efforts?
<--- Score

43. What is your decision requirements diagram?
<--- Score

44. Is the solution technically practical?
<--- Score

45. What current systems have to be understood and/or changed?
<--- Score

46. What lessons, if any, from a pilot were incorporated into the design of the full-scale solution?
<--- Score

47. How does the team improve its work?
<--- Score

48. Are risk management tasks balanced centrally and locally?
<--- Score

49. Are risk triggers captured?
<--- Score

50. How do you manage and improve your firewall services work systems to deliver customer value and achieve organizational success and sustainability?
<--- Score

51. Does the goal represent a desired result that can be measured?

<--- Score

52. To what extent does management recognize firewall services as a tool to increase the results?
<--- Score

53. Is there any other firewall services solution?
<--- Score

54. What tools were used to evaluate the potential solutions?
<--- Score

55. How will you recognize and celebrate results?
<--- Score

56. Would you develop a firewall services Communication Strategy?
<--- Score

57. What strategies for firewall services improvement are successful?
<--- Score

58. Who will be responsible for making the decisions to include or exclude requested changes once firewall services is underway?
<--- Score

59. Explorations of the frontiers of firewall services will help you build influence, improve firewall services, optimize decision making, and sustain change, what is your approach?
<--- Score

60. How do you manage firewall services risk?

<--- Score

61. What are your current levels and trends in key measures or indicators of workforce and leader development?
<--- Score

62. How do you define the solutions' scope?
<--- Score

63. Risk Identification: What are the possible risk events your organization faces in relation to firewall services?
<--- Score

64. How do you measure risk?
<--- Score

65. What is the implementation plan?
<--- Score

66. How will you know that you have improved?
<--- Score

67. What area needs the greatest improvement?
<--- Score

68. What is firewall services risk?
<--- Score

69. Who are the firewall services decision-makers?
<--- Score

70. How do the firewall services results compare with the performance of your competitors and other organizations with similar offerings?

<--- Score

71. Who are the key stakeholders for the firewall services evaluation?

<--- Score

72. What firewall services improvements can be made?

<--- Score

73. Have you identified breakpoints and/or risk tolerances that will trigger broad consideration of a potential need for intervention or modification of strategy?

<--- Score

74. Where do the firewall services decisions reside?

<--- Score

75. Are the most efficient solutions problem-specific?

<--- Score

76. Is the firewall services risk managed?

<--- Score

77. How can you improve firewall services?

<--- Score

78. Who should make the firewall services decisions?

<--- Score

79. What should a proof of concept or pilot accomplish?

<--- Score

80. Do you cover the five essential competencies: Communication, Collaboration,Innovation, Adaptability, and Leadership that improve an organizations ability to leverage the new firewall services in a volatile global economy?
<--- Score

81. How can you improve performance?
<--- Score

82. For decision problems, how do you develop a decision statement?
<--- Score

83. What actually has to improve and by how much?
<--- Score

84. Is the scope clearly documented?
<--- Score

85. What were the underlying assumptions on the cost-benefit analysis?
<--- Score

86. Is supporting firewall services documentation required?
<--- Score

87. What is the risk?
<--- Score

88. How do you measure improved firewall services service perception, and satisfaction?
<--- Score

89. Can the solution be designed and implemented within an acceptable time period?
<--- Score

90. What were the criteria for evaluating a firewall services pilot?
<--- Score

91. How does your organization evaluate strategic firewall services success?
<--- Score

92. Risk factors: what are the characteristics of firewall services that make it risky?
<--- Score

93. At what point will vulnerability assessments be performed once firewall services is put into production (e.g., ongoing Risk Management after implementation)?
<--- Score

94. What do you want to improve?
<--- Score

95. Who makes the firewall services decisions in your organization?
<--- Score

96. How are firewall services risks managed?
<--- Score

97. Which firewall services solution is appropriate?
<--- Score

98. Who manages firewall services risk?

<--- Score

99. What are the expected firewall services results?
<--- Score

100. Why improve in the first place?
<--- Score

101. How is knowledge sharing about risk management improved?
<--- Score

102. What is the team's contingency plan for potential problems occurring in implementation?
<--- Score

103. Where do you need firewall services improvement?
<--- Score

104. Do you combine technical expertise with business knowledge and firewall services Key topics include lifecycles, development approaches, requirements and how to make a business case?
<--- Score

105. What is firewall services's impact on utilizing the best solution(s)?
<--- Score

106. How do you decide how much to remunerate an employee?
<--- Score

107. How risky is your organization?
<--- Score

108. Are you assessing firewall services and risk?
<--- Score

109. When you map the key players in your own work and the types/domains of relationships with them, which relationships do you find easy and which challenging, and why?
<--- Score

110. Who controls the risk?
<--- Score

111. How will you know when its improved?
<--- Score

112. Does a good decision guarantee a good outcome?
<--- Score

113. Are procedures documented for managing firewall services risks?
<--- Score

114. Who controls key decisions that will be made?
<--- Score

115. What risks do you need to manage?
<--- Score

116. Do you have the optimal project management team structure?
<--- Score

117. Is there a high likelihood that any recommendations will achieve their intended results?

<--- Score

118. What practices helps your organization to develop its capacity to recognize patterns?
<--- Score

119. Who are the firewall services decision makers?
<--- Score

120. How do you deal with firewall services risk?
<--- Score

121. Was a firewall services charter developed?
<--- Score

122. What are the implications of the one critical firewall services decision 10 minutes, 10 months, and 10 years from now?
<--- Score

123. Which of the recognised risks out of all risks can be most likely transferred?
<--- Score

124. How will you know that a change is an improvement?
<--- Score

125. What are the affordable firewall services risks?
<--- Score

126. What tools do you use once you have decided on a firewall services strategy and more importantly how do you choose?
<--- Score

127. How do you keep improving firewall services?
<--- Score

128. Is any firewall services documentation required?
<--- Score

129. What to do with the results or outcomes of measurements?
<--- Score

130. How are policy decisions made and where?
<--- Score

Add up total points for this section:
_____ = Total points for this section

Divided by: _____ (number of statements answered) = _____
Average score for this section

Transfer your score to the firewall services Index at the beginning of the Self-Assessment.

CRITERION #6: CONTROL:

INTENT: Implement the practical
solution. Maintain the performance and
correct possible complications.

In my belief, the answer to this
question is clearly defined:

5 Strongly Agree

4 Agree

3 Neutral

2 Disagree

1 Strongly Disagree

1. What are the critical parameters to watch?
<--- Score

2. What is the control/monitoring plan?
<--- Score

3. Is knowledge gained on process shared and
institutionalized?
<--- Score

4. Against what alternative is success being measured?

<--- Score

5. Is there a firewall services Communication plan covering who needs to get what information when?

<--- Score

6. Does firewall services appropriately measure and monitor risk?

<--- Score

7. Do you monitor the effectiveness of your firewall services activities?

<--- Score

8. What key inputs and outputs are being measured on an ongoing basis?

<--- Score

9. What should you measure to verify efficiency gains?

<--- Score

10. How do you plan for the cost of succession?

<--- Score

11. What can you control?

<--- Score

12. What firewall services standards are applicable?

<--- Score

13. Do the firewall services decisions you make today help people and the planet tomorrow?

<--- Score

14. Are there documented procedures?
<--- Score

15. How will you measure your QA plan's effectiveness?
<--- Score

16. Are suggested corrective/restorative actions indicated on the response plan for known causes to problems that might surface?
<--- Score

17. Does the firewall services performance meet the customer's requirements?
<--- Score

18. What do you measure to verify effectiveness gains?
<--- Score

19. How do senior leaders actions reflect a commitment to the organizations firewall services values?
<--- Score

20. How will new or emerging customer needs/ requirements be checked/communicated to orient the process toward meeting the new specifications and continually reducing variation?
<--- Score

21. Where do ideas that reach policy makers and planners as proposals for firewall services strengthening and reform actually originate?

<--- Score

22. How might the group capture best practices and lessons learned so as to leverage improvements?
<--- Score

23. Who is the firewall services process owner?
<--- Score

24. Are operating procedures consistent?
<--- Score

25. What are the key elements of your firewall services performance improvement system, including your evaluation, organizational learning, and innovation processes?
<--- Score

26. What are your results for key measures or indicators of the accomplishment of your firewall services strategy and action plans, including building and strengthening core competencies?
<--- Score

27. Is there a standardized process?
<--- Score

28. How do you spread information?
<--- Score

29. Do the viable solutions scale to future needs?
<--- Score

30. How is change control managed?
<--- Score

31. Will any special training be provided for results interpretation?
<--- Score

32. How will input, process, and output variables be checked to detect for sub-optimal conditions?
<--- Score

33. Is new knowledge gained imbedded in the response plan?
<--- Score

34. How will the process owner verify improvement in present and future sigma levels, process capabilities?
<--- Score

35. Act/Adjust: What Do you Need to Do Differently?
<--- Score

36. What is the best design framework for firewall services organization now that, in a post industrial-age if the top-down, command and control model is no longer relevant?
<--- Score

37. How will the process owner and team be able to hold the gains?
<--- Score

38. How widespread is its use?
<--- Score

39. Will existing staff require re-training, for example, to learn new business processes?
<--- Score

40. Will the team be available to assist members in planning investigations?
<--- Score

41. Is reporting being used or needed?
<--- Score

42. Does a troubleshooting guide exist or is it needed?
<--- Score

43. Who sets the firewall services standards?
<--- Score

44. What is your plan to assess your security risks?
<--- Score

45. Has the firewall services value of standards been quantified?
<--- Score

46. Is there documentation that will support the successful operation of the improvement?
<--- Score

47. Is the firewall services test/monitoring cost justified?
<--- Score

48. Can support from partners be adjusted?
<--- Score

49. Are new process steps, standards, and documentation ingrained into normal operations?
<--- Score

50. Are the planned controls working?
<--- Score

51. What do your reports reflect?
<--- Score

52. Are the planned controls in place?
<--- Score

53. Are pertinent alerts monitored, analyzed and distributed to appropriate personnel?
<--- Score

54. Is there a recommended audit plan for routine surveillance inspections of firewall services's gains?
<--- Score

55. How will firewall services decisions be made and monitored?
<--- Score

56. Have new or revised work instructions resulted?
<--- Score

57. What other areas of the group might benefit from the firewall services team's improvements, knowledge, and learning?
<--- Score

58. How do your controls stack up?
<--- Score

59. Do you monitor the firewall services decisions made and fine tune them as they evolve?
<--- Score

60. How do you select, collect, align, and integrate firewall services data and information for tracking daily operations and overall organizational performance, including progress relative to strategic objectives and action plans?
<--- Score

61. What is the recommended frequency of auditing?
<--- Score

62. Does the response plan contain a definite closed loop continual improvement scheme (e.g., plan-do-check-act)?
<--- Score

63. Is a response plan established and deployed?
<--- Score

64. What are customers monitoring?
<--- Score

65. What are you attempting to measure/monitor?
<--- Score

66. What are the performance and scale of the firewall services tools?
<--- Score

67. Is there a control plan in place for sustaining improvements (short and long-term)?
<--- Score

68. Who is going to spread your message?
<--- Score

69. Are the firewall services standards challenging?

<--- Score

70. What should the next improvement project be that is related to firewall services?
<--- Score

71. Who controls critical resources?
<--- Score

72. Are controls in place and consistently applied?
<--- Score

73. Are you measuring, monitoring and predicting firewall services activities to optimize operations and profitability, and enhancing outcomes?
<--- Score

74. What is the standard for acceptable firewall services performance?
<--- Score

75. Are documented procedures clear and easy to follow for the operators?
<--- Score

76. In the case of a firewall services project, the criteria for the audit derive from implementation objectives, an audit of a firewall services project involves assessing whether the recommendations outlined for implementation have been met, can you track that any firewall services project is implemented as planned, and is it working?
<--- Score

77. What are the known security controls?
<--- Score

78. How can you best use all of your knowledge repositories to enhance learning and sharing?
<--- Score

79. Implementation Planning: is a pilot needed to test the changes before a full roll out occurs?
<--- Score

80. Is there a transfer of ownership and knowledge to process owner and process team tasked with the responsibilities.
<--- Score

81. How do controls support value?
<--- Score

82. Is a response plan in place for when the input, process, or output measures indicate an 'out-of-control' condition?
<--- Score

83. Is there an action plan in case of emergencies?
<--- Score

84. Who will be in control?
<--- Score

85. You may have created your quality measures at a time when you lacked resources, technology wasn't up to the required standard, or low service levels were the industry norm. Have those circumstances changed?
<--- Score

86. Who has control over resources?

<--- Score

87. How will report readings be checked to effectively monitor performance?
<--- Score

88. How will the day-to-day responsibilities for monitoring and continual improvement be transferred from the improvement team to the process owner?
<--- Score

89. How is firewall services project cost planned, managed, monitored?
<--- Score

90. What other systems, operations, processes, and infrastructures (hiring practices, staffing, training, incentives/rewards, metrics/dashboards/scorecards, etc.) need updates, additions, changes, or deletions in order to facilitate knowledge transfer and improvements?
<--- Score

91. Does job training on the documented procedures need to be part of the process team's education and training?
<--- Score

92. What quality tools were useful in the control phase?
<--- Score

93. Is there a documented and implemented monitoring plan?
<--- Score

94. How likely is the current firewall services plan to come in on schedule or on budget?
<--- Score

95. Will your goals reflect your program budget?
<--- Score

96. What adjustments to the strategies are needed?
<--- Score

97. How do you plan on providing proper recognition and disclosure of supporting companies?
<--- Score

98. Has the improved process and its steps been standardized?
<--- Score

Add up total points for this section:
_ _ _ _ _ = Total points for this section

Divided by: _ _ _ _ _ _ (number of statements answered) = _ _ _ _ _ _ Average score for this section

Transfer your score to the firewall services Index at the beginning of the Self-Assessment.

CRITERION #7: SUSTAIN:

INTENT: Retain the benefits.

In my belief, the answer to this question is clearly defined:

5 Strongly Agree

4 Agree

3 Neutral

2 Disagree

1 Strongly Disagree

1. What have you done to protect your business from competitive encroachment?
<--- Score

2. What is your BATNA (best alternative to a negotiated agreement)?
<--- Score

3. What unique value proposition (UVP) do you offer?
<--- Score

4. Do you have enough freaky customers in your portfolio pushing you to the limit day in and day out?
<--- Score

5. What is a feasible sequencing of reform initiatives over time?
<--- Score

6. Who is responsible for ensuring appropriate resources (time, people and money) are allocated to firewall services?
<--- Score

7. What is the craziest thing you can do?
<--- Score

8. Who is the main stakeholder, with ultimate responsibility for driving firewall services forward?
<--- Score

9. What happens when a new employee joins the organization?
<--- Score

10. Do you know who is a friend or a foe?
<--- Score

11. What threat is firewall services addressing?
<--- Score

12. Will there be any necessary staff changes (redundancies or new hires)?
<--- Score

13. What projects are going on in the organization today, and what resources are those projects using

from the resource pools?
<--- Score

14. How do you foster the skills, knowledge, talents, attributes, and characteristics you want to have?
<--- Score

15. Is your strategy driving your strategy? Or is the way in which you allocate resources driving your strategy?
<--- Score

16. What is the funding source for this project?
<--- Score

17. How will you insure seamless interoperability of firewall services moving forward?
<--- Score

18. What are the potential basics of firewall services fraud?
<--- Score

19. How will you ensure you get what you expected?
<--- Score

20. What trophy do you want on your mantle?
<--- Score

21. Which individuals, teams or departments will be involved in firewall services?
<--- Score

22. Is there any reason to believe the opposite of my current belief?
<--- Score

23. Operational - will it work?
<--- Score

24. Are you paying enough attention to the partners your company depends on to succeed?
<--- Score

25. How do you create buy-in?
<--- Score

26. Instead of going to current contacts for new ideas, what if you reconnected with dormant contacts-- the people you used to know? If you were going reactivate a dormant tie, who would it be?
<--- Score

27. What firewall services modifications can you make work for you?
<--- Score

28. If you do not follow, then how to lead?
<--- Score

29. Do you say no to customers for no reason?
<--- Score

30. Who is responsible for firewall services?
<--- Score

31. What is the overall talent health of your organization as a whole at senior levels, and for each organization reporting to a member of the Senior Leadership Team?
<--- Score

32. How do you engage the workforce, in addition to satisfying them?
<--- Score

33. How do senior leaders deploy your organizations vision and values through your leadership system, to the workforce, to key suppliers and partners, and to customers and other stakeholders, as appropriate?
<--- Score

34. How do you manage firewall services Knowledge Management (KM)?
<--- Score

35. What is the big firewall services idea?
<--- Score

36. What are you challenging?
<--- Score

37. What would have to be true for the option on the table to be the best possible choice?
<--- Score

38. Why is firewall services important for you now?
<--- Score

39. Do you see more potential in people than they do in themselves?
<--- Score

40. Who do we want your customers to become?
<--- Score

41. How can you become more high-tech but still be high touch?

<--- Score

42. Can you maintain your growth without detracting from the factors that have contributed to your success?

<--- Score

43. Have benefits been optimized with all key stakeholders?

<--- Score

44. Are assumptions made in firewall services stated explicitly?

<--- Score

45. Are the criteria for selecting recommendations stated?

<--- Score

46. How do you govern and fulfill your societal responsibilities?

<--- Score

47. What are the business goals firewall services is aiming to achieve?

<--- Score

48. How are you doing compared to your industry?

<--- Score

49. What is an unauthorized commitment?

<--- Score

50. Are there any activities that you can take off your to do list?

<--- Score

51. What have been your experiences in defining long range firewall services goals?
<--- Score

52. Political -is anyone trying to undermine this project?
<--- Score

53. What you are going to do to affect the numbers?
<--- Score

54. Are your responses positive or negative?
<--- Score

55. Who are your customers?
<--- Score

56. What is the kind of project structure that would be appropriate for your firewall services project, should it be formal and complex, or can it be less formal and relatively simple?
<--- Score

57. If you had to rebuild your organization without any traditional competitive advantages (i.e., no killer technology, promising research, innovative product/ service delivery model, etcetera), how would your people have to approach their work and collaborate together in order to create the necessary conditions for success?
<--- Score

58. If you weren't already in this business, would you enter it today? And if not, what are you going to do about it?

<--- Score

59. Are you relevant? Will you be relevant five years from now? Ten?
<--- Score

60. If you had to leave your organization for a year and the only communication you could have with employees/colleagues was a single paragraph, what would you write?
<--- Score

61. What stupid rule would you most like to kill?
<--- Score

62. Whose voice (department, ethnic group, women, older workers, etc) might you have missed hearing from in your company, and how might you amplify this voice to create positive momentum for your business?
<--- Score

63. Who do you want your customers to become?
<--- Score

64. What goals did you miss?
<--- Score

65. Do firewall services rules make a reasonable demand on a users capabilities?
<--- Score

66. What are the barriers to increased firewall services production?
<--- Score

67. Which firewall services goals are the most important?
<--- Score

68. If you find that you havent accomplished one of the goals for one of the steps of the firewall services strategy, what will you do to fix it?
<--- Score

69. Did your employees make progress today?
<--- Score

70. What are the success criteria that will indicate that firewall services objectives have been met and the benefits delivered?
<--- Score

71. How do you lead with firewall services in mind?
<--- Score

72. What are your personal philosophies regarding firewall services and how do they influence your work?
<--- Score

73. Who will manage the integration of tools?
<--- Score

74. Who is responsible for errors?
<--- Score

75. What may be the consequences for the performance of an organization if all stakeholders are not consulted regarding firewall services?
<--- Score

76. Why not do firewall services?
<--- Score

77. Can you do all this work?
<--- Score

78. How important is firewall services to the user organizations mission?
<--- Score

79. Who uses your product in ways you never expected?
<--- Score

80. What is your question? Why?
<--- Score

81. How likely is it that a customer would recommend your company to a friend or colleague?
<--- Score

82. How do you keep records, of what?
<--- Score

83. How do you stay inspired?
<--- Score

84. How can you become the company that would put you out of business?
<--- Score

85. How do you foster innovation?
<--- Score

86. Are you using a design thinking approach and integrating Innovation, firewall services Experience,

and Brand Value?

<--- Score

87. What do we do when new problems arise?

<--- Score

88. What is the source of the strategies for firewall services strengthening and reform?

<--- Score

89. How do you go about securing firewall services?

<--- Score

90. How do you maintain firewall services's Integrity?

<--- Score

91. What one word do you want to own in the minds of your customers, employees, and partners?

<--- Score

92. What did you miss in the interview for the worst hire you ever made?

<--- Score

93. Do you have the right capabilities and capacities?

<--- Score

94. Do you feel that more should be done in the firewall services area?

<--- Score

95. How will you know that the firewall services project has been successful?

<--- Score

96. Is a firewall services team work effort in place?
<--- Score

97. Are you making progress, and are you making progress as firewall services leaders?
<--- Score

98. Marketing budgets are tighter, consumers are more skeptical, and social media has changed forever the way we talk about firewall services, how do you gain traction?
<--- Score

99. Do you know what you are doing? And who do you call if you don't?
<--- Score

100. Were lessons learned captured and communicated?
<--- Score

101. Who, on the executive team or the board, has spoken to a customer recently?
<--- Score

102. What is something you believe that nearly no one agrees with you on?
<--- Score

103. What role does communication play in the success or failure of a firewall services project?
<--- Score

104. Would you rather sell to knowledgeable and informed customers or to uninformed customers?
<--- Score

105. How do you proactively clarify deliverables and firewall services quality expectations?
<--- Score

106. What new services of functionality will be implemented next with firewall services ?
<--- Score

107. Who will provide the final approval of firewall services deliverables?
<--- Score

108. Are you satisfied with your current role? If not, what is missing from it?
<--- Score

109. Ask yourself: how would you do this work if you only had one staff member to do it?
<--- Score

110. How do you accomplish your long range firewall services goals?
<--- Score

111. Why should people listen to you?
<--- Score

112. How do you make it meaningful in connecting firewall services with what users do day-to-day?
<--- Score

113. What are the rules and assumptions your industry operates under? What if the opposite were true?
<--- Score

114. What will be the consequences to the stakeholder (financial, reputation etc) if firewall services does not go ahead or fails to deliver the objectives?
<--- Score

115. What is the range of capabilities?
<--- Score

116. How do you track customer value, profitability or financial return, organizational success, and sustainability?
<--- Score

117. How much does firewall services help?
<--- Score

118. Is the firewall services organization completing tasks effectively and efficiently?
<--- Score

119. Do you think you know, or do you know you know ?
<--- Score

120. Have new benefits been realized?
<--- Score

121. What is effective firewall services?
<--- Score

122. What trouble can you get into?
<--- Score

123. How much contingency will be available in the

budget?

<--- Score

124. If there were zero limitations, what would you do differently?

<--- Score

125. What are the top 3 things at the forefront of your firewall services agendas for the next 3 years?

<--- Score

126. When information truly is ubiquitous, when reach and connectivity are completely global, when computing resources are infinite, and when a whole new set of impossibilities are not only possible, but happening, what will that do to your business?

<--- Score

127. How do you assess the firewall services pitfalls that are inherent in implementing it?

<--- Score

128. What potential megatrends could make your business model obsolete?

<--- Score

129. Is there any existing firewall services governance structure?

<--- Score

130. How is implementation research currently incorporated into each of your goals?

<--- Score

131. What management system can you use to

leverage the firewall services experience, ideas, and concerns of the people closest to the work to be done?

<--- Score

132. Why do and why don't your customers like your organization?

<--- Score

133. Is firewall services realistic, or are you setting yourself up for failure?

<--- Score

134. How do you transition from the baseline to the target?

<--- Score

135. Are you maintaining a past–present–future perspective throughout the firewall services discussion?

<--- Score

136. Who are the key stakeholders?

<--- Score

137. What firewall services skills are most important?

<--- Score

138. Who will determine interim and final deadlines?

<--- Score

139. Is it economical; do you have the time and money?

<--- Score

140. What counts that you are not counting?

<--- Score

141. What is the overall business strategy?
<--- Score

142. Who is on the team?
<--- Score

143. How do you determine the key elements that affect firewall services workforce satisfaction, how are these elements determined for different workforce groups and segments?
<--- Score

144. In a project to restructure firewall services outcomes, which stakeholders would you involve?
<--- Score

145. How does firewall services integrate with other stakeholder initiatives?
<--- Score

146. In the past year, what have you done (or could you have done) to increase the accurate perception of your company/brand as ethical and honest?
<--- Score

147. If your customer were your grandmother, would you tell her to buy what you're selling?
<--- Score

148. How do you know if you are successful?
<--- Score

149. Are the assumptions believable and achievable?
<--- Score

150. Is the impact that firewall services has shown?
<--- Score

151. How do customers see your organization?
<--- Score

152. At what moment would you think; Will I get fired?
<--- Score

153. Who have you, as a company, historically been when you've been at your best?
<--- Score

154. Do you have past firewall services successes?
<--- Score

155. If you were responsible for initiating and implementing major changes in your organization, what steps might you take to ensure acceptance of those changes?
<--- Score

156. Where can you break convention?
<--- Score

157. Is a firewall services breakthrough on the horizon?
<--- Score

158. What is your competitive advantage?
<--- Score

159. What are current firewall services paradigms?
<--- Score

160. In retrospect, of the projects that you pulled the plug on, what percent do you wish had been allowed to keep going, and what percent do you wish had ended earlier?
<--- Score

161. What information is critical to your organization that your executives are ignoring?
<--- Score

162. Who do you think the world wants your organization to be?
<--- Score

163. What was the last experiment you ran?
<--- Score

164. What happens if you do not have enough funding?
<--- Score

165. What would you recommend your friend do if he/she were facing this dilemma?
<--- Score

166. If your company went out of business tomorrow, would anyone who doesn't get a paycheck here care?
<--- Score

167. What is the purpose of firewall services in relation to the mission?
<--- Score

168. How do you ensure that implementations of firewall services products are done in a way that ensures safety?

<--- Score

169. What is the recommended frequency of auditing?
<--- Score

170. What are specific firewall services rules to follow?
<--- Score

171. What are the short and long-term firewall services goals?
<--- Score

172. What is the estimated value of the project?
<--- Score

173. Who will be responsible for deciding whether firewall services goes ahead or not after the initial investigations?
<--- Score

174. Why will customers want to buy your organizations products/services?
<--- Score

175. Is firewall services dependent on the successful delivery of a current project?
<--- Score

176. What are your most important goals for the strategic firewall services objectives?
<--- Score

177. Do you think firewall services accomplishes the goals you expect it to accomplish?

<--- Score

178. Whom among your colleagues do you trust, and for what?
<--- Score

179. How do you keep the momentum going?
<--- Score

180. Who are four people whose careers you have enhanced?
<--- Score

181. What are you trying to prove to yourself, and how might it be hijacking your life and business success?
<--- Score

182. What should you stop doing?
<--- Score

183. Is your basic point _____ or _____?
<--- Score

184. What is your firewall services strategy?
<--- Score

185. Why should you adopt a firewall services framework?
<--- Score

186. What knowledge, skills and characteristics mark a good firewall services project manager?
<--- Score

187. Are new benefits received and understood?

<--- Score

188. How do you set firewall services stretch targets and how do you get people to not only participate in setting these stretch targets but also that they strive to achieve these?
<--- Score

189. If you got fired and a new hire took your place, what would she do different?
<--- Score

190. Is there a work around that you can use?
<--- Score

191. What business benefits will firewall services goals deliver if achieved?
<--- Score

192. Do you have an implicit bias for capital investments over people investments?
<--- Score

193. What are the long-term firewall services goals?
<--- Score

194. What are the essentials of internal firewall services management?
<--- Score

195. How can you negotiate firewall services successfully with a stubborn boss, an irate client, or a deceitful coworker?
<--- Score

196. What are the key enablers to make this firewall services move?

<--- Score

197. What is your formula for success in firewall services ?

<--- Score

198. Are all key stakeholders present at all Structured Walkthroughs?

<--- Score

199. What are the challenges?

<--- Score

200. Who else should you help?

<--- Score

201. How can you incorporate support to ensure safe and effective use of firewall services into the services that you provide?

<--- Score

202. What are the usability implications of firewall services actions?

<--- Score

203. What is it like to work for you?

<--- Score

204. How do you listen to customers to obtain actionable information?

<--- Score

205. Will it be accepted by users?

<--- Score

206. Is maximizing firewall services protection the same as minimizing firewall services loss?

<--- Score

207. How do you deal with firewall services changes?

<--- Score

208. What happens at your organization when people fail?

<--- Score

209. What does your signature ensure?

<--- Score

210. Can you break it down?

<--- Score

211. Can the schedule be done in the given time?

<--- Score

212. How will you motivate the stakeholders with the least vested interest?

<--- Score

213. Are you / should you be revolutionary or evolutionary?

<--- Score

214. What are the gaps in your knowledge and experience?

<--- Score

215. What must you excel at?

<--- Score

Add up total points for this section:
_____ = Total points for this section

Divided by: _____ (number of
statements answered) = _____
Average score for this section

Transfer your score to the firewall
services Index at the beginning of the
Self-Assessment.

Firewall Services and Managing Projects, Criteria for Project Managers:

1.0 Initiating Process Group: Firewall Services

1. How well did the chosen processes produce the expected results?

2. What are the short and long term implications?

3. Did the Firewall Services project team have the right skills?

4. How is each deliverable reviewed, verified, and validated?

5. Information sharing?

6. What communication items need improvement?

7. How can you make your needs known?

8. Were resources available as planned?

9. Are identified risks being monitored properly, are new risks arising during the Firewall Services project or are foreseen risks occurring?

10. For technology Firewall Services projects only: Are all production support stakeholders (Business unit, technical support, & user) prepared for implementation with appropriate contingency plans?

11. What were things that you did very well and want to do the same again on the next Firewall Services project?

12. What are the overarching issues of your organization?

13. How to control and approve each phase?

14. Specific - is the objective clear in terms of what, how, when, and where the situation will be changed?

15. Were decisions made in a timely manner?

16. Realistic - are the desired results expressed in a way that the team will be motivated and believe that the required level of involvement will be obtained?

17. Just how important is your work to the overall success of the Firewall Services project?

18. At which stage, in a typical Firewall Services project do stake holders have maximum influence?

1.1 Project Charter: Firewall Services

19. Are you building in-house ?

20. For whom?

21. What is the business need?

22. Why executive support?

23. How will you know a change is an improvement?

24. Are there special technology requirements?

25. Why is it important?

26. When is a charter needed?

27. Firewall Services project objective statement: what must the Firewall Services project do?

28. Review the general mission What system will be affected by the improvement efforts?

29. What are the assigned resources?

30. Why is a Firewall Services project Charter used?

31. Who manages integration?

32. How are Firewall Services projects different from operations?

33. What material?

34. What are you trying to accomplish?

35. What are the known stakeholder requirements?

36. Why have you chosen the aim you have set forth?

37. Firewall Services project deliverables: what is the Firewall Services project going to produce?

38. What are the constraints?

1.2 Stakeholder Register: Firewall Services

39. How much influence do they have on the Firewall Services project?

40. Who is managing stakeholder engagement?

41. Who wants to talk about Security?

42. How big is the gap?

43. What & Why?

44. Who are the stakeholders?

45. What is the power of the stakeholder?

46. How should employers make voices heard?

47. Is your organization ready for change?

48. What opportunities exist to provide communications?

49. What are the major Firewall Services project milestones requiring communications or providing communications opportunities?

50. How will reports be created?

1.3 Stakeholder Analysis Matrix: Firewall Services

51. What actions can be taken to reduce or mitigate risk?

52. Lack of competitive strength?

53. What are the mechanisms of public and social accountability, and how can they be made better?

54. Which conditions out of the control of the management are crucial to contribute for the achievement of the development objective?

55. Information and research?

56. Loss of key staff?

57. Industry or lifestyle trends?

58. Competitor intentions - various?

59. Participatory approach: how will key stakeholders participate in the Firewall Services project?

60. Why involve the stakeholder?

61. Legislative effects?

62. Marketing - reach, distribution, awareness?

63. Could any of your organizations weaknesses

seriously threaten development?

64. Philosophy and values?

65. If the baseline is now, and if its improved it will be better than now?

66. Who is most dependent on the resources at stake?

67. Are the interests in line with the program objectives?

68. What should thwe organizations stakeholders avoid?

69. Resources, assets, people?

70. Cultural, attitudinal, behavioural?

2.0 Planning Process Group: Firewall Services

71. What is involved in Firewall Services project scope management, and why is good Firewall Services project scope management so important on information technology Firewall Services projects?

72. How well defined and documented are the Firewall Services project management processes you chose to use?

73. Will the products created live up to the necessary quality?

74. Are work methodologies, financial instruments, etc. shared among departments, organizations and Firewall Services projects?

75. If you are late, will anybody notice?

76. How should needs be met?

77. What type of estimation method are you using?

78. To what extent and in what ways are the Firewall Services project contributing to progress towards organizational reform?

79. What will you do to minimize the impact should a risk event occur?

80. How are it Firewall Services projects different?

81. Explanation: is what the Firewall Services project intents to solve a hard question?

82. How will you do it?

83. You did your readings, yes?

84. To what extent are the visions and actions of the partners consistent or divergent with regard to the program?

85. If action is called for, what form should it take?

86. Are there efficient coordination mechanisms to avoid overloading the counterparts, participating stakeholders?

87. How do you integrate Firewall Services project Planning with the Iterative/Evolutionary SDLC?

88. What is the critical path for this Firewall Services project, and what is the duration of the critical path?

89. Is the duration of the program sufficient to ensure a cycle that will Firewall Services project the sustainability of the interventions?

90. Why is it important to determine activity sequencing on Firewall Services projects?

2.1 Project Management Plan: Firewall Services

91. Is the budget realistic?

92. Are alternatives safe, functional, constructible, economical, reasonable and sustainable?

93. Who is the Firewall Services project Manager?

94. Who is the sponsor?

95. Why Change?

96. If the Firewall Services project management plan is a comprehensive document that guides you in Firewall Services project execution and control, then what should it NOT contain?

97. What went wrong?

98. How can you best help your organization to develop consistent practices in Firewall Services project management planning stages?

99. Are calculations and results of analyzes essentially correct?

100. Is the engineering content at a feasibility level-of-detail, and is it sufficiently complete, to provide an adequate basis for the baseline cost estimate?

101. Is mitigation authorized or recommended?

102. Are there any client staffing expectations?

103. Are cost risk analysis methods applied to develop contingencies for the estimated total Firewall Services project costs?

104. What went right?

105. Are comparable cost estimates used for comparing, screening and selecting alternative plans, and has a reasonable cost estimate been developed for the recommended plan?

106. How well are you able to manage your risk?

107. What is risk management?

2.2 Scope Management Plan: Firewall Services

108. What is the need the Firewall Services project will address?

109. What are the risks of not having good inter-organization cooperation on the Firewall Services project?

110. Pop quiz – which are the same inputs as in scope planning?

111. Are decisions captured in a decisions log?

112. Is each item clearly and completely defined?

113. Have the procedures for identifying variances from estimates & adjusting the detailed work program been followed?

114. What are the risks that could significantly affect the communication on the Firewall Services project?

115. Are internal Firewall Services project status meetings held at reasonable intervals?

116. Are post milestone Firewall Services project reviews (PMPR) conducted with your organization at least once a year?

117. Is the steering committee active in Firewall Services project oversight?

118. Can each item be appropriately scheduled?

119. Has the business need been clearly defined?

120. Are assumptions being identified, recorded, analyzed, qualified and closed?

121. Timeline and milestones?

122. What strengths do you have?

123. Are Firewall Services project leaders committed to this Firewall Services project full time?

124. Where do scope management processes fit in?

125. Are the people assigned to the Firewall Services project sufficiently qualified?

126. Are vendor invoices audited for accuracy before payment?

127. How relevant is this attribute to this Firewall Services project or audit?

2.3 Requirements Management Plan: Firewall Services

128. Which hardware or software, related to, or as outcome of the Firewall Services project is new to your organization?

129. After the requirements are gathered and set forth on the requirements register, theyre little more than a laundry list of items. Some may be duplicates, some might conflict with others and some will be too broad or too vague to understand. Describe how the requirements will be analyzed. Who will perform the analysis?

130. What is a problem?

131. If it exists, where is it housed?

132. Who is responsible for quantifying the Firewall Services project requirements?

133. Who is responsible for monitoring and tracking the Firewall Services project requirements?

134. Who came up with this requirement?

135. Should you include sub-activities?

136. Is any organizational data being used or stored?

137. Did you distinguish the scope of work the contractor(s) will be required to do?

138. Do you really need to write this document at all?

139. How will you communicate scheduled tasks to other team members?

140. Do you have price sheets and a methodology for determining the total proposal cost?

141. How detailed should the Firewall Services project get?

142. Who will perform the analysis?

143. Are actual resource expenditures versus planned still acceptable?

144. Is infrastructure setup part of your Firewall Services project?

145. How will bidders price evaluations be done, by deliverables, phases, or in a big bang?

146. Will the Firewall Services project requirements become approved in writing?

147. Will you use an assessment of the Firewall Services project environment as a tool to discover risk to the requirements process?

2.4 Requirements Documentation: Firewall Services

148. How to document system requirements?

149. How does what is being described meet the business need?

150. Are there legal issues?

151. What facilities must be supported by the system?

152. How much does requirements engineering cost?

153. What can tools do for us?

154. What are the acceptance criteria?

155. Who is interacting with the system?

156. Can the requirement be changed without a large impact on other requirements?

157. The problem with gathering requirements is right there in the word gathering. What images does it conjure?

158. How linear / iterative is your Requirements Gathering process (or will it be)?

159. What is effective documentation?

160. How will they be documented / shared?

161. If applicable; are there issues linked with the fact that this is an offshore Firewall Services project?

162. Basic work/business process; high-level, what is being touched?

163. How much testing do you need to do to prove that your system is safe?

164. How do you get the user to tell you what they want?

165. Does your organization restrict technical alternatives?

166. Does the system provide the functions which best support the customers needs?

167. Can the requirements be checked?

2.5 Requirements Traceability Matrix: Firewall Services

168. Is there a requirements traceability process in place?

169. How will it affect the stakeholders personally in career?

170. How small is small enough?

171. What is the WBS?

172. What percentage of Firewall Services projects are producing traceability matrices between requirements and other work products?

173. Why do you manage scope?

174. What are the chronologies, contingencies, consequences, criteria?

175. Do you have a clear understanding of all subcontracts in place?

176. Describe the process for approving requirements so they can be added to the traceability matrix and Firewall Services project work can be performed. Will the Firewall Services project requirements become approved in writing?

177. Why use a WBS?

178. Will you use a Requirements Traceability Matrix?

179. How do you manage scope?

2.6 Project Scope Statement: Firewall Services

180. How often will scope changes be reviewed?

181. Have you been able to easily identify success criteria and create objective measurements for each of the Firewall Services project scopes goal statements?

182. Have you been able to thoroughly document the Firewall Services projects assumptions and constraints?

183. Has a method and process for requirement tracking been developed?

184. Are the input requirements from the team members clearly documented and communicated?

185. Will the risk status be reported to management on a regular and frequent basis?

186. What are the possible consequences should a risk come to occur?

187. Is there a Change Management Board?

188. Will there be a Change Control Process in place?

189. Risks?

190. How often do you estimate that the scope might

change, and why?

191. Is the plan under configuration management?

192. What is a process you might recommend to verify the accuracy of the research deliverable?

193. Elements of scope management that deal with concept development ?

194. Is your organization structure appropriate for the Firewall Services projects size and complexity?

195. Will tasks be marked complete only after QA has been successfully completed?

196. What actions will be taken to mitigate the risk?

197. Is the quality function identified and assigned?

198. If you were to write a list of what should not be included in the scope statement, what are the things that you would recommend be described as out-of-scope?

2.7 Assumption and Constraint Log: Firewall Services

199. How relevant is this attribute to this Firewall Services project or audit?

200. Is the amount of effort justified by the anticipated value of forming a new process?

201. When can log be discarded?

202. Have all necessary approvals been obtained?

203. Have Firewall Services project management standards and procedures been established and documented?

204. Diagrams and tables are included to account for complex concepts and increase overall readability?

205. Contradictory information between different documents?

206. What other teams / processes would be impacted by changes to the current process, and how?

207. Is this model reasonable?

208. Are there cosmetic errors that hinder readability and comprehension?

209. What is positive about the current process?

210. Have all involved stakeholders and work groups committed to the Firewall Services project?

211. No superfluous information or marketing narrative?

212. What do you log?

213. Are processes for release management of new development from coding and unit testing, to integration testing, to training, and production defined and followed?

214. Were the system requirements formally reviewed prior to initiating the design phase?

215. How are new requirements or changes to requirements identified?

216. Should factors be unpredictable over time?

217. Are funding and staffing resource estimates sufficiently detailed and documented for use in planning and tracking the Firewall Services project?

218. Can the requirements be traced to the appropriate components of the solution, as well as test scripts?

2.8 Work Breakdown Structure: Firewall Services

219. Where does it take place?

220. How big is a work-package?

221. How much detail?

222. What is the probability of completing the Firewall Services project in less that xx days?

223. Why is it useful?

224. Is it a change in scope?

225. When does it have to be done?

226. Why would you develop a Work Breakdown Structure?

227. How far down?

228. What is the probability that the Firewall Services project duration will exceed xx weeks?

229. How will you and your Firewall Services project team define the Firewall Services projects scope and work breakdown structure?

230. Who has to do it?

231. When do you stop?

232. Do you need another level?

233. What has to be done?

234. Is the work breakdown structure (wbs) defined and is the scope of the Firewall Services project clear with assigned deliverable owners?

2.9 WBS Dictionary: Firewall Services

235. Contemplated overhead expenditure for each period based on the best information currently available?

236. Are procedures established to prevent changes to the contract budget base other than the already stated authorized by contractual action?

237. Are your organizations and items of cost assigned to each pool identified?

238. Is cost and schedule performance measurement done in a consistent, systematic manner?

239. How many levels?

240. Are records maintained to show how management reserves are used?

241. Time-phased control account budgets?

242. Does the contractors system provide for the determination of cost variances attributable to the excess usage of material?

243. Changes in the overhead pool and/or organization structures?

244. Detailed schedules which support control account and work package start and completion dates/events?

245. Is the work done on a work package level as described in the WBS dictionary?

246. The anticipated business volume?

247. Are meaningful indicators identified for use in measuring the status of cost and schedule performance?

248. Identify and isolate causes of favorable and unfavorable cost and schedule variances?

249. Is work progressively subdivided into detailed work packages as requirements are defined?

250. Are the responsibilities and authorities of each of the above organizational elements or managers clearly defined?

251. Is the anticipated (firm and potential) business base Firewall Services projected in a rational, consistent manner?

252. Are overhead cost budgets established for each organization which has authority to incur overhead costs?

2.10 Schedule Management Plan: Firewall Services

253. Are schedule performance measures defined including pre-set triggers for specific actions?

254. Are procurement deliverables arriving on time and to specification?

255. Are the processes for status updates and maintenance defined?

256. Have Firewall Services project team accountabilities & responsibilities been clearly defined?

257. Are the activity durations realistic and at an appropriate level of detail for effective management?

258. Has the Firewall Services project scope been baselined?

259. Have external dependencies been captured in the schedule?

260. Does a documented Firewall Services project organizational policy & plan (i.e. governance model) exist?

261. Has the ims been resource-loaded and are assigned resources reasonable and available?

262. Are the Firewall Services project team members

located locally to the users/stakeholders?

263. Do all stakeholders know how to access this repository and where to find the Firewall Services project documentation?

264. Are any non-compliance issues that exist due to your organizations practices communicated to your organization?

265. Have activity relationships and interdependencies within tasks been adequately identified?

266. Are internal Firewall Services project status meetings held at reasonable intervals?

267. Firewall Services project definition & scope?

268. What tools and techniques will be used to estimate activity durations?

269. Are scheduled deliverables actually delivered?

270. Are the processes for schedule assessment and analysis defined?

271. Are actuals compared against estimates to analyze and correct variances?

272. Is the schedule vertically and horizontally traceable?

2.11 Activity List: Firewall Services

273. In what sequence?

274. Can you determine the activity that must finish, before this activity can start?

275. Is there anything planned that does not need to be here?

276. For other activities, how much delay can be tolerated?

277. What is the total time required to complete the Firewall Services project if no delays occur?

278. What are the critical bottleneck activities?

279. How difficult will it be to do specific activities on this Firewall Services project?

280. How do you determine the late start (LS) for each activity?

281. Who will perform the work?

282. How should ongoing costs be monitored to try to keep the Firewall Services project within budget?

283. The wbs is developed as part of a joint planning session. and how do you know that youhave done this right?

284. What is the LF and LS for each activity?

285. Is infrastructure setup part of your Firewall Services project?

286. When will the work be performed?

287. When do the individual activities need to start and finish?

288. How detailed should a Firewall Services project get?

289. What went well?

290. What did not go as well?

291. Where will it be performed?

2.12 Activity Attributes: Firewall Services

292. Have constraints been applied to the start and finish milestones for the phases?

293. What is the general pattern here?

294. Time for overtime?

295. Where else does it apply?

296. Would you consider either of corresponding activities an outlier?

297. What is missing?

298. Is there a trend during the year?

299. Resources to accomplish the work?

300. Are the required resources available?

301. How difficult will it be to do specific activities on this Firewall Services project?

302. Were there other ways you could have organized the data to achieve similar results?

303. Activity: fair or not fair?

304. How else could the items be grouped?

305. Which method produces the more accurate cost assignment?

306. What is your organizations history in doing similar activities?

307. Why?

308. Do you feel very comfortable with your prediction?

309. How many resources do you need to complete the work scope within a limit of X number of days?

310. Have you identified the Activity Leveling Priority code value on each activity?

2.13 Milestone List: Firewall Services

311. How late can each activity be finished and started?

312. How will you get the word out to customers?

313. Own known vulnerabilities?

314. Competitive advantages?

315. Who will manage the Firewall Services project on a day-to-day basis?

316. How do you manage time?

317. What date will the task finish?

318. It is to be a narrative text providing the crucial aspects of your Firewall Services project proposal answering what, who, how, when and where?

319. Milestone pages should display the UserID of the person who added the milestone. Does a report or query exist that provides this audit information?

320. When will the Firewall Services project be complete?

321. Usps (unique selling points)?

322. Global influences?

323. What is the market for your technology, product

or service?

324. Identify critical paths (one or more) and which activities are on the critical path?

325. Do you foresee any technical risks or developmental challenges?

326. What are your competitors vulnerabilities?

327. How soon can the activity start?

2.14 Network Diagram: Firewall Services

328. If a current contract exists, can you provide the vendor name, contract start, and contract expiration date?

329. If x is long, what would be the completion time if you break x into two parallel parts of y weeks and z weeks?

330. What are the Key Success Factors?

331. What activities must follow this activity?

332. What controls the start and finish of a job?

333. What are the Major Administrative Issues?

334. Are the gantt chart and/or network diagram updated periodically and used to assess the overall Firewall Services project timetable?

335. Which type of network diagram allows you to depict four types of dependencies?

336. What is the completion time?

337. What activities must occur simultaneously with this activity?

338. How difficult will it be to do specific activities on this Firewall Services project?

339. Planning: who, how long, what to do?

340. Are you on time?

341. Where do you schedule uncertainty time?

342. What job or jobs precede it?

343. What job or jobs could run concurrently?

344. Exercise: what is the probability that the Firewall Services project duration will exceed xx weeks?

345. What activity must be completed immediately before this activity can start?

2.15 Activity Resource Requirements: Firewall Services

346. Why do you do that?

347. Do you use tools like decomposition and rolling-wave planning to produce the activity list and other outputs?

348. Are there unresolved issues that need to be addressed?

349. What are constraints that you might find during the Human Resource Planning process?

350. How many signatures do you require on a check and does this match what is in your policy and procedures?

351. Which logical relationship does the PDM use most often?

352. Other support in specific areas?

353. How do you handle petty cash?

354. What is the Work Plan Standard?

355. Organizational Applicability?

356. When does monitoring begin?

357. Anything else?

2.16 Resource Breakdown Structure: Firewall Services

358. What is the difference between % Complete and % work?

359. What is each stakeholders desired outcome for the Firewall Services project?

360. Why do you do it?

361. Which resources should be in the resource pool?

362. How should the information be delivered?

363. Who delivers the information?

364. Who needs what information?

365. How difficult will it be to do specific activities on this Firewall Services project?

366. The list could probably go on, but, the thing that you would most like to know is, How long & How much?

367. Changes based on input from stakeholders?

368. Who will use the system?

369. Is predictive resource analysis being done?

370. What defines a successful Firewall Services

project?

371. What is Firewall Services project communication management?

372. What are the requirements for resource data?

373. What is the purpose of assigning and documenting responsibility?

374. What is the primary purpose of the human resource plan?

2.17 Activity Duration Estimates: Firewall Services

375. Why is it important to determine activity sequencing on Firewall Services projects?

376. Did anything besides luck make a difference between success and failure?

377. Firewall Services project manager has received activity duration estimates from his team. Which does one need in order to complete schedule development?

378. Why is activity definition the first process involved in Firewall Services project time management?

379. What do you think about the WBSs for them?

380. Which tips for taking the PMP exam do you think would be most helpful for you?

381. Are activity dependencies identified?

382. Are contractor costs, schedule and technical performance monitored throughout the Firewall Services project?

383. How does poking fun at technical professionals communications skills impact the industry and educational programs?

384. How do theories relate to Firewall Services project management?

385. Which would be the NEXT thing for the Firewall Services project manager to do?

386. Consider the history of modern quality management. How have experts such as Deming, Juran, Crosby, and Taguchi affected the quality movement and todays use of Six Sigma?

387. Do you think many information technology professionals have experience writing RFPs and evaluating proposals for information technology Firewall Services projects?

388. Research recruiting and retention strategies at three different companies. What distinguishes one organization from another in this area?

389. Will the new application negatively affect the current IT infrastructure?

390. What is done after activity duration estimation?

391. What is the duration of the critical path for this Firewall Services project?

392. Are Firewall Services project costs tracked in the general ledger?

393. How does a Firewall Services project life cycle differ from a product life cycle?

394. How is the Firewall Services project doing?

2.18 Duration Estimating Worksheet: Firewall Services

395. Value pocket identification & quantification what are value pockets?

396. What is cost and Firewall Services project cost management?

397. How can the Firewall Services project be displayed graphically to better visualize the activities?

398. Small or large Firewall Services project?

399. Is the Firewall Services project responsive to community need?

400. What is your role?

401. Will the Firewall Services project collaborate with the local community and leverage resources?

402. When, then?

403. What questions do you have?

404. What is next?

405. Define the work as completely as possible. What work will be included in the Firewall Services project?

406. Done before proceeding with this activity or what can be done concurrently?

407. When does your organization expect to be able to complete it?

408. Is this operation cost effective?

409. Is a construction detail attached (to aid in explanation)?

410. What work will be included in the Firewall Services project?

411. What utility impacts are there?

2.19 Project Schedule: Firewall Services

412. What is Firewall Services project management?

413. How do you know that youhave done this right?

414. Activity charts and bar charts are graphical representations of a Firewall Services project schedule ...how do they differ?

415. Why is this particularly bad?

416. Was the Firewall Services project schedule reviewed by all stakeholders and formally accepted?

417. Did the final product meet or exceed user expectations?

418. Is the structure for tracking the Firewall Services project schedule well defined and assigned to a specific individual?

419. Your Firewall Services project management plan results in a Firewall Services project schedule that is too long. If the Firewall Services project network diagram cannot change and you have extra personnel resources, what is the BEST thing to do?

420. Eliminate unnecessary activities. Are there activities that came from a template or previous Firewall Services project that are not applicable on this phase of this Firewall Services project?

421. How much slack is available in the Firewall Services project?

422. Are key risk mitigation strategies added to the Firewall Services project schedule?

423. Change management required?

424. If you can not fix it, how do you do it differently?

425. How do you manage Firewall Services project Risk?

426. Why time management?

427. What is risk?

428. Are the original Firewall Services project schedule and budget realistic?

429. Verify that the update is accurate. Are all remaining durations correct?

430. Meet requirements?

2.20 Cost Management Plan: Firewall Services

431. Are target dates established for each milestone deliverable?

432. Weve met your goals?

433. Is it standard practice to formally commit stakeholders to the Firewall Services project via agreements?

434. Have all unresolved risks been documented?

435. Who will prepare the cost estimates?

436. Progress measurement and control – How will the Firewall Services project measure and control progress?

437. Cost / benefit analysis?

438. Are status reports received per the Firewall Services project Plan?

439. Contingency – how will cost contingency be administered?

440. Is there a formal set of procedures supporting Issues Management?

441. Have lessons learned been conducted after each Firewall Services project release?

442. Are the Firewall Services project team members located locally to the users/stakeholders?

443. Are the key elements of a Firewall Services project Charter present?

444. Time management – how will the schedule impact of changes be estimated and approved?

445. Who should write the PEP?

446. Have the key elements of a coherent Firewall Services project management strategy been established?

447. Are issues raised, assessed, actioned, and resolved in a timely and efficient manner?

448. Are quality inspections and review activities listed in the Firewall Services project schedule(s)?

449. Cost tracking and performance analysis – How will cost tracking and performance analysis be accomplished?

450. Alignment to strategic goals & objectives?

2.21 Activity Cost Estimates: Firewall Services

451. What is a Firewall Services project Management Plan?

452. Will you need to provide essential services information about activities?

453. Scope statement only direct or indirect costs as well?

454. How do you allocate indirect costs to activities?

455. Does the activity rely on a common set of tools to carry it out?

456. What defines a successful Firewall Services project?

457. Vac -variance at completion, how much over/ under budget do you expect to be?

458. What cost data should be used to estimate costs during the 2-year follow-up period?

459. Review – what are some common errors in activities to avoid?

460. What areas were overlooked on this Firewall Services project?

461. How and when do you enter into Firewall

Services project Procurement Management?

462. Where can you get activity reports?

463. What is the activity inventory?

464. What is your organizations history in doing similar tasks?

465. Estimated cost?

466. How do you change activities?

467. Can you change your activities?

468. What were things that you did very well and want to do the same again on the next Firewall Services project?

469. How do you fund change orders?

470. Were sponsors and decision makers available when needed outside regularly scheduled meetings?

2.22 Cost Estimating Worksheet: Firewall Services

471. What info is needed?

472. Does the Firewall Services project provide innovative ways for stakeholders to overcome obstacles or deliver better outcomes?

473. Who is best positioned to know and assist in identifying corresponding factors?

474. Is it feasible to establish a control group arrangement?

475. What is the estimated labor cost today based upon this information?

476. What additional Firewall Services project(s) could be initiated as a result of this Firewall Services project?

477. What will others want?

478. What happens to any remaining funds not used?

479. What can be included?

480. What costs are to be estimated?

481. Will the Firewall Services project collaborate with the local community and leverage resources?

482. Can a trend be established from historical

performance data on the selected measure and are the criteria for using trend analysis or forecasting methods met?

483. Identify the timeframe necessary to monitor progress and collect data to determine how the selected measure has changed?

484. What is the purpose of estimating?

485. How will the results be shared and to whom?

486. Ask: are others positioned to know, are others credible, and will others cooperate?

487. Is the Firewall Services project responsive to community need?

2.23 Cost Baseline: Firewall Services

488. Are there contingencies or conditions related to the acceptance?

489. Verify business objectives. Are others appropriate, and well-articulated?

490. Where do changes come from?

491. Have all the product or service deliverables been accepted by the customer?

492. Have the lessons learned been filed with the Firewall Services project Management Office?

493. Does it impact schedule, cost, quality?

494. Review your risk triggers -have your risks changed?

495. Are you asking management for something as a result of this update?

496. Are you meeting with your team regularly?

497. Does a process exist for establishing a cost baseline to measure Firewall Services project performance?

498. How do you manage cost?

499. What deliverables come first?

500. Why do you manage cost?

501. Has the actual cost of the Firewall Services project (or Firewall Services project phase) been tallied and compared to the approved budget?

502. What do you want to measure ?

503. Who will use corresponding metrics ?

504. Is request in line with priorities?

505. Escalation criteria met?

506. Have the actual milestone completion dates been compared to the approved schedule?

2.24 Quality Management Plan: Firewall Services

507. Where do you focus?

508. How does your organization make it easy for customers to seek assistance or complain?

509. Have all stakeholders been identified?

510. How do your action plans support the strategic objectives?

511. Who is responsible?

512. Is there a Quality Management Plan?

513. How does your organization recruit, hire, and retain new employees?

514. What is the Difference Between a QMP and QAPP?

515. You know what your customers expectations are regarding this process?

516. How are changes to procedures made?

517. Is the steering committee active in Firewall Services project oversight?

518. Are decisions/actions based on data collected?

519. Checking the completeness and appropriateness of the sampling and testing. Were the right locations/ samples tested for the right parameters?

520. Does the program use other agents to collect samples?

521. Sampling part of task?

522. List your organizations customer contact standards that employees are expected to maintain. How are corresponding standards measured?

523. How do senior leaders create and communicate values and performance expectations?

524. How does your organization ensure the reliability, accuracy, timeliness, security and accessibility of data and information?

525. What is the Quality Management Plan?

526. Do trained quality assurance auditors conduct the audits as defined in the Quality Management Plan and scheduled by the Firewall Services project manager?

2.25 Quality Metrics: Firewall Services

527. What happens if you get an abnormal result?

528. Which are the right metrics to use?

529. Has risk analysis been adequately reviewed?

530. Have risk areas been identified?

531. Are there already quality metrics available that detect nonlinear embeddings and trends similar to the users perception?

532. Is there a set of procedures to capture, analyze and act on quality metrics?

533. Can visual measures help you to filter visualizations of interest?

534. What if the biggest risk to your business were the already stated people who do not complain?

535. What method of measurement do you use?

536. What documentation is required?

537. Did evaluation start on time?

538. Are quality metrics defined?

539. What does this tell us?

540. Filter visualizations of interest?

541. Does risk analysis documentation meet standards?

542. How do you calculate corresponding metrics?

543. How is it being measured?

544. Was the overall quality better or worse than previous products?

545. Is there alignment within your organization on definitions?

2.26 Process Improvement Plan: Firewall Services

546. Has the time line required to move measurement results from the points of collection to databases or users been established?

547. Who should prepare the process improvement action plan?

548. Everyone agrees on what process improvement is, right?

549. The motive is determined by asking, Why do you want to achieve this goal?

550. Are you making progress on the goals?

551. What personnel are the champions for the initiative?

552. What is the test-cycle concept?

553. Where are you now?

554. How do you measure?

555. Why do you want to achieve the goal?

556. What is quality and how will you ensure it?

557. Modeling current processes is great, and will you ever see a return on that investment?

558. Are you following the quality standards?

559. Where do you want to be?

560. What personnel are the sponsors for that initiative?

561. Have the supporting tools been developed or acquired?

562. Have storage and access mechanisms and procedures been determined?

563. How do you manage quality?

564. Does explicit definition of the measures exist?

565. What is the return on investment?

2.27 Responsibility Assignment Matrix: Firewall Services

566. Do managers and team members provide helpful suggestions during review meetings?

567. Will too many Signing-off responsibilities delay the completion of the activity/deliverable?

568. Is budgeted cost for work performed calculated in a manner consistent with the way work is planned?

569. Does the contractors system provide unit or lot costs when applicable?

570. Where does all this information come from?

571. Who is responsible for work and budgets for each wbs?

572. No rs: if a task has no one listed as responsible, who is getting the job done?

573. Is the anticipated (firm and potential) business base Firewall Services projected in a rational, consistent manner?

574. Wbs elements contractually specified for reporting of status (lowest level only)?

575. What does wbs accomplish?

576. How do you manage remotely to staff in other

Divisions?

577. Do others have the time to dedicate to your Firewall Services project?

578. Does the Firewall Services project need to be analyzed further to uncover additional responsibilities?

579. The staff characteristics – is the group or the person capable to work together as a team?

580. Evaluate the impact of schedule changes, work around, etc?

581. Changes in the current direct and Firewall Services projected base?

582. Do work packages consist of discrete tasks which are adequately described?

583. Are people encouraged to bring up issues?

584. Is work properly classified as measured effort, LOE, or apportioned effort and appropriately separated?

585. Ideas for developing soft skills at your organization?

2.28 Roles and Responsibilities: Firewall Services

586. What is working well?

587. Concern: where are you limited or have no authority, where you can not influence?

588. Required skills, knowledge, experience?

589. What specific behaviors did you observe?

590. Are Firewall Services project team roles and responsibilities identified and documented?

591. What should you highlight for improvement?

592. What is working well within your organizations performance management system?

593. What expectations were met?

594. What expectations were NOT met?

595. Was the expectation clearly communicated?

596. How well did the Firewall Services project Team understand the expectations of specific roles and responsibilities?

597. Do the values and practices inherent in the culture of your organization foster or hinder the process?

598. Be specific; avoid generalities. Thank you and great work alone are insufficient. What exactly do you appreciate and why?

599. What should you do now to prepare yourself for a promotion, increased responsibilities or a different job?

600. Influence: what areas of organizational decision making are you able to influence when you do not have authority to make the final decision?

601. To decide whether to use a quality measurement, ask how will you know when it is achieved?

602. Accountabilities: what are the roles and responsibilities of individual team members?

603. Who is responsible for implementation activities and where will the functions, roles and responsibilities be defined?

2.29 Human Resource Management Plan: Firewall Services

604. Are staff skills known and available for each task?

605. Who is involved?

606. Personnel with expertise?

607. Are software metrics formally captured, analyzed and used as a basis for other Firewall Services project estimates?

608. How are you going to ensure that you have a well motivated workforce?

609. Are internal Firewall Services project status meetings held at reasonable intervals?

610. Has a structured approach been used to break work effort into manageable components (WBS)?

611. Who needs training?

612. Are the payment terms being followed?

613. What is the boss?

614. Have process improvement efforts been completed before requirements efforts begin?

615. Are changes in deliverable commitments agreed to by all affected groups & individuals?

616. Have the key functions and capabilities been defined and assigned to each release or iteration?

617. How to convince to employees that it is a necessary process?

618. Are changes in scope (deliverable commitments) agreed to by all affected groups & individuals?

619. Is the current culture aligned with the vision, mission, and values of the department?

620. Responsiveness to change and the resulting demands for different skills and abilities?

621. Has your organization readiness assessment been conducted?

2.30 Communications Management Plan: Firewall Services

622. Do you then often overlook a key stakeholder or stakeholder group?

623. Will messages be directly related to the release strategy or phases of the Firewall Services project?

624. How were corresponding initiatives successful?

625. How will the person responsible for executing the communication item be notified?

626. Why is stakeholder engagement important?

627. What approaches to you feel are the best ones to use?

628. Are there potential barriers between the team and the stakeholder?

629. What is the stakeholders level of authority?

630. Are others part of the communications management plan?

631. Who needs to know and how much?

632. Which stakeholders are thought leaders, influences, or early adopters?

633. How much time does it take to do it?

634. What steps can you take for a positive relationship?

635. How is this initiative related to other portfolios, programs, or Firewall Services projects?

636. Why do you manage communications?

637. Timing: when do the effects of the communication take place?

638. Who have you worked with in past, similar initiatives?

639. What communications method?

2.31 Risk Management Plan: Firewall Services

640. Does the Firewall Services project have the authority and ability to avoid the risk?

641. How is risk monitoring performed?

642. Do you manage the process through use of metrics?

643. Risk categories: what are the main categories of risks that should be addressed on this Firewall Services project?

644. Could others have been better mitigated?

645. For software; does the software interface with new or unproven hardware or unproven vendor products?

646. Are the metrics meaningful and useful?

647. Litigation – what is the probability that lawsuits will cause problems or delays in the Firewall Services project?

648. Management -what contingency plans do you have if the risk becomes a reality?

649. What other risks are created by choosing an avoidance strategy?

650. Do you have a consistent repeatable process that is actually used?

651. Do you train all developers in the process?

652. Risks should be identified during which phase of Firewall Services project management life cycle?

653. Are tool mentors available?

654. How is risk identification performed?

655. Are the software tools integrated with each other?

656. Was an original risk assessment/risk management plan completed?

657. How quickly does each item need to be resolved?

658. What is the likelihood that your organization would accept responsibility for the risk?

659. Degree of confidence in estimated size estimate?

2.32 Risk Register: Firewall Services

660. What action, if any, has been taken to respond to the risk?

661. How could corresponding Risk affect the Firewall Services project in terms of cost and schedule?

662. What should you do now?

663. Amongst the action plans and recommendations that you have to introduce are there some that could stop or delay the overall program?

664. What is the appropriate level of risk management for this Firewall Services project?

665. What is the reason for current performance gaps and do the risks and opportunities identified previously account for this?

666. Can the likelihood and impact of failing to achieve corresponding recommendations and action plans be assessed?

667. What evidence do you have to justify the likelihood score of the risk (audit, incident report, claim, complaints, inspection, internal review)?

668. Who is going to do it?

669. Having taken action, how did the responses effect change, and where is the Firewall Services project now?

670. How often will the Risk Management Plan and Risk Register be formally reviewed, and by whom?

671. How are risks identified?

672. Assume the event happens, what is the Most Likely impact?

673. What are the assumptions and current status that support the assessment of the risk?

674. Contingency actions - planned actions to reduce the immediate seriousness of the risk when it does occur. What should you do when?

675. What could prevent you delivering on the strategic program objectives and what is being done to mitigate corresponding issues?

676. Assume the risk event or situation happens, what would the impact be?

677. Financial risk -can your organization afford to undertake the Firewall Services project?

678. Are there any knock-on effects/impact on any of the other areas?

679. What risks might negatively or positively affect achieving the Firewall Services project objectives?

2.33 Probability and Impact Assessment: Firewall Services

680. Does the Firewall Services project team have experience with the technology to be implemented?

681. Is the process supported by tools?

682. What are the probabilities of chosen technologies being suitable for local conditions?

683. What is the likelihood?

684. Which functions, departments, and activities of your organization are going to be affected?

685. How well is the risk understood?

686. Are there alternative opinions/solutions/ processes you should explore?

687. Do you use any methods to analyze risks?

688. Can it be enlarged by drawing people from other areas of your organization?

689. How do risks change during a Firewall Services project life cycle?

690. Do you use diagramming techniques to show cause and effect?

691. What are the current or emerging trends of

culture?

692. Monitoring of the overall Firewall Services project status – are there any changes in the Firewall Services project that can effect and cause new possible risks?

693. Which risks need to move on to Perform Quantitative Risk Analysis?

694. How risk averse are you?

695. What will be the impact or consequence if the risk occurs?

696. What risks does your organization have if the Firewall Services projects fail to meet deadline?

697. What is the impact if the risk does occur?

698. Has something like this been done before?

699. Are there any Firewall Services projects similar to this one in existence?

2.34 Probability and Impact Matrix: Firewall Services

700. Risk may be made during which step of risk management?

701. Are the risk data complete?

702. What is the industrial relations prevailing in this organization?

703. Were there any Firewall Services projects similar to this one in existence?

704. During which risk management process is a determination to transfer a risk made?

705. What is the probability of the risk occurring?

706. Do you have specific methods that you use for each phase of the process?

707. What should you do FIRST?

708. Are testing tools available and suitable?

709. Is the number of people on the Firewall Services project team adequate to do the job?

710. Several experts are offsite, and wish to be included. How can this be done?

711. Do end-users have realistic expectations?

712. What will be the likely political situation during the life of the Firewall Services project?

713. What are data sources?

714. How realistic is the timing of introduction?

715. Do others match with the clients requirement?

716. Is the present organizational structure for handling the Firewall Services project sufficient?

2.35 Risk Data Sheet: Firewall Services

717. What can happen?

718. What are you weak at and therefore need to do better?

719. How reliable is the data source?

720. Has a sensitivity analysis been carried out?

721. What are the main threats to your existence?

722. What is the environment within which you operate (social trends, economic, community values, broad based participation, national directions etc.)?

723. What are your core values?

724. Potential for recurrence?

725. How can it happen?

726. What will be the consequences if the risk happens?

727. What was measured?

728. What were the Causes that contributed?

729. Type of risk identified?

730. Do effective diagnostic tests exist?

731. What are you trying to achieve (Objectives)?

732. What actions can be taken to eliminate or remove risk?

733. If it happens, what are the consequences?

734. Has the most cost-effective solution been chosen?

735. During work activities could hazards exist?

2.36 Procurement Management Plan: Firewall Services

736. Do Firewall Services project teams & team members report on status / activities / progress?

737. Are written status reports provided on a designated frequent basis?

738. Is the steering committee active in Firewall Services project oversight?

739. How long will it take for the purchase cost to be the same as the lease cost?

740. Has a quality assurance plan been developed for the Firewall Services project?

741. Are risk triggers captured?

742. Based on your Firewall Services project communication management plan, what worked well?

743. Are decisions made in a timely manner?

744. What is a Firewall Services project Management Plan?

745. Public engagement – did you get it right?

746. Does the Firewall Services project team have the right skills?

747. Is it standard practice to formally commit stakeholders to the Firewall Services project via agreements?

748. Are governance roles and responsibilities documented?

749. How will you coordinate Procurement with aspects of the Firewall Services project?

750. Was the scope definition used in task sequencing?

751. Are adequate resources provided for the quality assurance function?

752. Are the quality tools and methods identified in the Quality Plan appropriate to the Firewall Services project?

753. What is the last item a Firewall Services project manager must do to finalize Firewall Services project close-out?

2.37 Source Selection Criteria: Firewall Services

754. Team leads: what is your process for assigning ratings?

755. How should the oral presentations be handled?

756. How can solicitation Schedules be improved to yield more effective price competition?

757. Who is entitled to a debriefing?

758. How is past performance evaluated?

759. Can you identify proposed teaming partners and/or subcontractors and consider the nature and extent of proposed involvement in satisfying the Firewall Services project requirements?

760. Has all proposal data been loaded?

761. What should clarifications include?

762. Who must be notified?

763. What source selection software is your team using?

764. What can not be disclosed?

765. Do proposed hours support content and schedule?

766. Is the contracting office likely to receive more purchase requests for this item or service during the coming year?

767. Are types/quantities of material, facilities appropriate?

768. If the costs are normalized, please account for how the normalization is conducted. Is a cost realism analysis used?

769. How do you ensure an integrated assessment of proposals?

770. How should comments received in response to a RFP be handled?

771. How do you manage procurement?

772. What should a DRFP include?

773. With the rapid changes in information technology, will media be readable in five or ten years?

2.38 Stakeholder Management Plan: Firewall Services

774. Do Firewall Services project teams & team members report on status / activities / progress?

775. What guidelines or procedures currently exist that must be adhered to (eg departmental accounting procedures)?

776. Where are the verification requirements to be documented (eg purchase order, agreement etc)?

777. What preventative action can be taken to reduce the likelihood a risk will be realised?

778. What is the process for purchases that arent acceptable (eg damaged goods)?

779. Were Firewall Services project team members involved in detailed estimating and scheduling?

780. What is meant by activity dependencies and how do they relate to network diagramming?

781. Were Firewall Services project team members involved in the development of activity & task decomposition?

782. Has a sponsor been identified?

783. Have the key elements of a coherent Firewall Services project management strategy been

established?

784. Was trending evident between audits?

785. What is the general purpose in defining responsibilities of the already stated affiliated with the Firewall Services project?

786. What process was used to identify risks to the Firewall Services projects success?

787. Has the budget been baselined?

788. Are Firewall Services project team members involved in detailed estimating and scheduling?

789. Are formal code reviews conducted?

790. Is staff trained on the software technologies that are being used on the Firewall Services project?

2.39 Change Management Plan: Firewall Services

791. What new behaviours are required?

792. Who is responsible for which tasks?

793. What new roles are needed?

794. Different application of an existing process?

795. Who will be the change levers?

796. Is there an adequate supply of people for the new roles?

797. Is there a support model for this application and are the details available for distribution?

798. Has the training co-ordinator been provided with the training details and put in place the necessary arrangements?

799. Have the systems been configured and tested?

800. How can you best frame the message so that it addresses the audiences interests?

801. Will the readiness criteria be met prior to the training roll out?

802. Has a training need analysis been carried out?

803. What tasks are needed?

804. Is it the same for each of the business units?

805. What are the current methods of sharing information and do there need to be new ones developed?

806. Would you need to tailor a special message for each segment of the audience?

807. What do you expect the target audience to do, say, think or feel as a result of this communication?

808. When does it make sense to customize?

809. What risks may occur upfront?

810. Who might present the most resistance?

3.0 Executing Process Group: Firewall Services

811. Measurable - are the targets measurable?

812. What are the main processes included in Firewall Services project quality management?

813. How do you enter durations, link tasks, and view critical path information?

814. How does the job market and current state of the economy affect human resource management?

815. Do the partners have sufficient financial capacity to keep up the benefits produced by the programme?

816. How does Firewall Services project management relate to other disciplines?

817. Do the products created live up to the necessary quality?

818. What factors are contributing to progress or delay in the achievement of products and results?

819. Will a new application be developed using existing hardware, software, and networks?

820. When will the Firewall Services project be done?

821. If a risk event occurs, what will you do?

822. How can software assist in Firewall Services project communications?

823. What are the critical steps involved with strategy mapping?

824. Is the program supported by national and/or local organizations?

825. How can your organization use a weighted decision matrix to evaluate proposals as part of source selection?

826. What business situation is being addressed?

827. How do you prevent staff are just doing busywork to pass the time?

828. What does it mean to take a systems view of a Firewall Services project?

829. What are deliverables of your Firewall Services project?

3.1 Team Member Status Report: Firewall Services

830. What specific interest groups do you have in place?

831. What is to be done?

832. How it is to be done?

833. Are your organizations Firewall Services projects more successful over time?

834. How does this product, good, or service meet the needs of the Firewall Services project and your organization as a whole?

835. When a teams productivity and success depend on collaboration and the efficient flow of information, what generally fails them?

836. Why is it to be done?

837. Do you have an Enterprise Firewall Services project Management Office (EPMO)?

838. Does the product, good, or service already exist within your organization?

839. Are the attitudes of staff regarding Firewall Services project work improving?

840. The problem with Reward & Recognition

Programs is that the truly deserving people all too often get left out. How can you make it practical?

841. How can you make it practical?

842. Does your organization have the means (staff, money, contract, etc.) to produce or to acquire the product, good, or service?

843. Will the staff do training or is that done by a third party?

844. How much risk is involved?

845. Is there evidence that staff is taking a more professional approach toward management of your organizations Firewall Services projects?

846. How will resource planning be done?

847. Does every department have to have a Firewall Services project Manager on staff?

848. Are the products of your organizations Firewall Services projects meeting customers objectives?

3.2 Change Request: Firewall Services

849. When to submit a change request?

850. Who has responsibility for approving and ranking changes?

851. How well do experienced software developers predict software change?

852. Will new change requests be acknowledged in a timely manner?

853. What has an inspector to inspect and to check?

854. How does a team identify the discrete elements of a configuration?

855. Will there be a change request form in use?

856. Has the change been highlighted and documented in the CSCI?

857. Have scm procedures for noting the change, recording it, and reporting it been followed?

858. Since there are no change requests in your Firewall Services project at this point, what must you have before you begin?

859. How are the measures for carrying out the change established?

860. What are the requirements for urgent changes?

861. Does the schedule include Firewall Services project management time and change request analysis time?

862. Will all change requests and current status be logged?

863. How to get changes (code) out in a timely manner?

864. Why control change across the life cycle?

865. Who needs to approve change requests?

866. How fast will change requests be approved?

867. Who is included in the change control team?

3.3 Change Log: Firewall Services

868. Is the change backward compatible without limitations?

869. Is this a mandatory replacement?

870. How does this relate to the standards developed for specific business processes?

871. How does this change affect the timeline of the schedule?

872. Is the change request open, closed or pending?

873. When was the request approved?

874. Is the change request within Firewall Services project scope?

875. Do the described changes impact on the integrity or security of the system?

876. Does the suggested change request represent a desired enhancement to the products functionality?

877. When was the request submitted?

878. Who initiated the change request?

879. Does the suggested change request seem to represent a necessary enhancement to the product?

880. Is the submitted change a new change or a

modification of a previously approved change?

881. Will the Firewall Services project fail if the change request is not executed?

882. Is the requested change request a result of changes in other Firewall Services project(s)?

883. Should a more thorough impact analysis be conducted?

884. How does this change affect scope?

3.4 Decision Log: Firewall Services

885. Which variables make a critical difference?

886. How do you define success?

887. How does provision of information, both in terms of content and presentation, influence acceptance of alternative strategies?

888. It becomes critical to track and periodically revisit both operational effectiveness; Are you noticing all that you need to, and are you interpreting what you see effectively?

889. What is the average size of your matters in an applicable measurement?

890. Adversarial environment. is your opponent open to a non-traditional workflow, or will it likely challenge anything you do?

891. Who will be given a copy of this document and where will it be kept?

892. What are the cost implications?

893. How does the use a Decision Support System influence the strategies/tactics or costs?

894. At what point in time does loss become unacceptable?

895. What makes you different or better than others

companies selling the same thing?

896. What eDiscovery problem or issue did your organization set out to fix or make better?

897. Linked to original objective?

898. Do strategies and tactics aimed at less than full control reduce the costs of management or simply shift the cost burden?

899. How does an increasing emphasis on cost containment influence the strategies and tactics used?

900. Behaviors; what are guidelines that the team has identified that will assist them with getting the most out of team meetings?

901. With whom was the decision shared or considered?

902. Is your opponent open to a non-traditional workflow, or will it likely challenge anything you do?

903. How effective is maintaining the log at facilitating organizational learning?

904. What is the line where eDiscovery ends and document review begins?

3.5 Quality Audit: Firewall Services

905. Has a written procedure been established to identify devices during all stages of receipt, reconditioning, distribution and installation so that mix-ups are prevented?

906. Statements of intent remain exactly that until they are put into effect. The next step is to deploy the already stated intentions. In other words, do the plans happen in reality?

907. Is the reports overall tone appropriate?

908. How does your organization know that its Governance system is appropriately effective and constructive?

909. What are your supplier audits?

910. Are complaint files maintained?

911. What does an analysis of your organizations staff profile suggest in terms of its planning, and how is this being addressed?

912. How does your organization know that its systems for meeting staff extracurricular learning support requirements are appropriately effective and constructive?

913. How does your organization know that its research funding systems are appropriately effective and constructive in enabling quality research

outcomes?

914. How does your organization know that its teaching activities (and staff learning) are effectively and constructively enhanced by its activities?

915. How does your organization know that its system for staff performance planning and review is appropriately effective and constructive?

916. How does your organization know that its system for attending to the health and wellbeing of its staff is appropriately effective and constructive?

917. How does your organization know that its system for recruiting the best staff possible are appropriately effective and constructive?

918. How does your organization know that its relationship with its (past) staff is appropriately effective and constructive?

919. What is the collective experience of the team to be assigned to an audit?

920. Will the evidence likely be sufficient and appropriate?

921. Can your organization demonstrate exactly how and why results were achieved?

922. Quality is about improvement and accountability. The immediate questions that arise out of that statement are: (i) improvement on what, and (ii) accountable to whom?

923. Are multiple statements on the same issue consistent with each other?

924. Are adequate and conveniently located toilet facilities available for use by the employees?

3.6 Team Directory: Firewall Services

925. Where should the information be distributed?

926. Contract requirements complied with?

927. Is construction on schedule?

928. Who will be the stakeholders on your next Firewall Services project?

929. Process decisions: are there any statutory or regulatory issues relevant to the timely execution of work?

930. What are you going to deliver or accomplish?

931. Why is the work necessary?

932. Process decisions: which organizational elements and which individuals will be assigned management functions?

933. Who are the Team Members?

934. Days from the time the issue is identified?

935. How does the team resolve conflicts and ensure tasks are completed?

936. When does information need to be distributed?

937. How do unidentified risks impact the outcome of the Firewall Services project?

938. Who will report Firewall Services project status to all stakeholders?

939. How will you accomplish and manage the objectives?

940. Process decisions: are all start-up, turn over and close out requirements of the contract satisfied?

941. Who are your stakeholders (customers, sponsors, end users, team members)?

942. When will you produce deliverables?

3.7 Team Operating Agreement: Firewall Services

943. Do you listen for voice tone and word choice to understand the meaning behind words?

944. What is the number of cases currently teamed?

945. Are there more than two functional areas represented by your team?

946. Are team roles clearly defined and accepted?

947. Did you prepare participants for the next meeting?

948. Must your members collaborate successfully to complete Firewall Services projects?

949. What types of accommodations will be formulated and put in place for sustaining the team?

950. Confidentiality: how will confidential information be handled?

951. Are there the right people on your team?

952. How will you resolve conflict efficiently and respectfully?

953. Do you begin with a question to engage everyone?

954. Do you prevent individuals from dominating the meeting?

955. How do you want to be thought of and known within your organization?

956. Do you send out the agenda and meeting materials in advance?

957. Do you brief absent members after they view meeting notes or listen to a recording?

958. The method to be used in the decision making process; Will it be consensus, majority rule, or the supervisor having the final say?

959. How will your group handle planned absences?

960. Do you solicit member feedback about meetings and what would make them better?

961. To whom do you deliver your services?

3.8 Team Performance Assessment: Firewall Services

962. Do friends perform better than acquaintances?

963. How much interpersonal friction is there in your team?

964. How hard did you try to make a good selection?

965. To what degree do members understand and articulate the same purpose without relying on ambiguous abstractions?

966. To what degree are the skill areas critical to team performance present?

967. To what degree will the approach capitalize on and enhance the skills of all team members in a manner that takes into consideration other demands on members of the team?

968. To what degree can team members frequently and easily communicate with one another?

969. To what degree do team members articulate the teams work approach?

970. How do you recognize and praise members for contributions?

971. To what degree will the team ensure that all members equitably share the work essential to the

success of the team?

972. To what degree are the members clear on what they are individually responsible for and what they are jointly responsible for?

973. To what degree does the teams purpose constitute a broader, deeper aspiration than just accomplishing short-term goals?

974. If you are worried about method variance before you collect data, what sort of design elements might you include to reduce or eliminate the threat of method variance?

975. To what degree do members articulate the goals beyond the team membership?

976. What are you doing specifically to develop the leaders around you?

977. To what degree are the goals ambitious?

978. What structural changes have you made or are you preparing to make?

979. To what degree does the teams work approach provide opportunity for members to engage in open interaction?

980. How do you encourage members to learn from each other?

981. Do you promptly inform members about major developments that may affect them?

3.9 Team Member Performance Assessment: Firewall Services

982. Are there any safeguards to prevent intentional or unintentional rating errors?

983. Where can team members go for more detailed information on performance measurement and assessment?

984. To what degree can team members meet frequently enough to accomplish the teams ends?

985. How are assessments designed, delivered, and otherwise used to maximize training?

986. What were the challenges that resulted for training and assessment?

987. Does platform-specific assessment information contribute to training placement or tailoring of instruction (e.g. aptitude-treatment interaction)?

988. Why do performance reviews?

989. How does your team work together?

990. Is it clear how goals will be accomplished?

991. What happens if a team member disagrees with the Job Expectations?

992. Does the rater (supervisor) have to wait for the

interim or final performance assessment review to tell an employee that the employees performance is unsatisfactory?

993. What, if any, steps are available for employees who feel they have been unfairly or inaccurately rated?

994. Do the goals support your organizations goals?

995. What is a significant fact or event?

996. What innovations (if any) are developed to realize goals?

997. What kinds of performance factors / elements do you use?

998. How will they be formed?

3.10 Issue Log: Firewall Services

999. Are there common objectives between the team and the stakeholder?

1000. What would have to change?

1001. Who reported the issue?

1002. What is the stakeholders political influence?

1003. Is the issue log kept in a safe place?

1004. Who is involved as you identify stakeholders?

1005. What steps can you take for positive relationships?

1006. Persistence; will users learn a work around or will they be bothered every time?

1007. What effort will a change need?

1008. Why do you manage human resources?

1009. Is access to the Issue Log controlled?

1010. What help do you and your team need from the stakeholders?

1011. What is the status of the issue?

1012. How is this initiative related to other portfolios, programs, or Firewall Services projects?

1013. What is a Stakeholder?

4.0 Monitoring and Controlling Process Group: Firewall Services

1014. How many more potential communications channels were introduced by the discovery of the new stakeholders?

1015. How do you monitor progress?

1016. Were escalated issues resolved promptly?

1017. What is the expected monetary value of the Firewall Services project?

1018. Is the program making progress in helping to achieve the set results?

1019. How will staff learn how to use the deliverables?

1020. Use: how will they use the information?

1021. How many potential communications channels exist on the Firewall Services project?

1022. Who are the Firewall Services project stakeholders?

1023. What is the timeline for the Firewall Services project?

1024. Have operating capacities been created and/or reinforced in partners?

1025. Is the program in place as intended?

1026. Overall, how does the program function to serve the clients?

1027. Is there sufficient time allotted between the general system design and the detailed system design phases?

1028. How is agile portfolio management done?

1029. Did you implement the program as designed?

4.1 Project Performance Report: Firewall Services

1030. To what degree does the teams purpose contain themes that are particularly meaningful and memorable?

1031. To what degree can team members vigorously define the teams purpose in considerations with others who are not part of the functioning team?

1032. To what degree can the team ensure that all members are individually and jointly accountable for the teams purpose, goals, approach, and work-products?

1033. To what degree are sub-teams possible or necessary?

1034. What is the PRS?

1035. To what degree does the informal organization make use of individual resources and meet individual needs?

1036. To what degree is there centralized control of information sharing?

1037. To what degree does the information network provide individuals with the information they require?

1038. To what degree do team members feel that the purpose of the team is important, if not exciting?

1039. To what degree do team members understand one anothers roles and skills?

1040. To what degree do team members agree with the goals, relative importance, and the ways in which achievement will be measured?

1041. To what degree does the information network communicate information relevant to the task?

1042. To what degree does the formal organization make use of individual resources and meet individual needs?

1043. To what degree do the structures of the formal organization motivate taskrelevant behavior and facilitate task completion?

1044. To what degree are the demands of the task compatible with and converge with the mission and functions of the formal organization?

1045. What is the degree to which rules govern information exchange between individuals within your organization?

1046. To what degree is the team cognizant of small wins to be celebrated along the way?

4.2 Variance Analysis: Firewall Services

1047. Are all cwbs elements specified for external reporting?

1048. Is there a logical explanation for any variance?

1049. Do you identify potential or actual budget-based and time-based schedule variances?

1050. Can the contractor substantiate work package and planning package budgets?

1051. How does the use of a single conversion element (rather than the traditional labor and overhead elements) affect standard costing?

1052. Did a new competitor enter the market?

1053. Does the accounting system provide a basis for auditing records of direct costs chargeable to the contract?

1054. Favorable or unfavorable variance?

1055. Is the anticipated (firm and potential) business base Firewall Services projected in a rational, consistent manner?

1056. Wbs elements contractually specified for reporting of status to your organization (lowest level only)?

1057. Budgeted cost for work performed?

1058. What is the total budget for the Firewall Services project (including estimates for authorized and unpriced work)?

1059. Is data disseminated to the contractors management timely, accurate, and usable?

1060. Are indirect costs accumulated for comparison with the corresponding budgets?

1061. Are data elements reconcilable between internal summary reports and reports forwarded to the stakeholders?

1062. How are variances affected by multiple material and labor categories?

1063. Does the scheduling system identify in a timely manner the status of work?

1064. Are overhead cost budgets established for each department which has authority to incur overhead costs?

1065. What costs are avoidable if one or more customers are dropped?

4.3 Earned Value Status: Firewall Services

1066. How does this compare with other Firewall Services projects?

1067. Validation is a process of ensuring that the developed system will actually achieve the stakeholders desired outcomes; Are you building the right product? What do you validate?

1068. Verification is a process of ensuring that the developed system satisfies the stakeholders agreements and specifications; Are you building the product right? What do you verify?

1069. How much is it going to cost by the finish?

1070. When is it going to finish?

1071. Where is evidence-based earned value in your organization reported?

1072. Are you hitting your Firewall Services projects targets?

1073. What is the unit of forecast value?

1074. Where are your problem areas?

1075. Earned value can be used in almost any Firewall Services project situation and in almost any Firewall Services project environment. it may be used on large

Firewall Services projects, medium sized Firewall Services projects, tiny Firewall Services projects (in cut-down form), complex and simple Firewall Services projects and in any market sector. some people, of course, know all about earned value, they have used it for years - but perhaps not as effectively as they could have?

1076. If earned value management (EVM) is so good in determining the true status of a Firewall Services project and Firewall Services project its completion, why is it that hardly any one uses it in information systems related Firewall Services projects?

4.4 Risk Audit: Firewall Services

1077. How do you manage risk?

1078. Are end-users enthusiastically committed to the Firewall Services project and the system/product to be built?

1079. Who is responsible for what?

1080. How are risk appetites expressed?

1081. Do your financial policies and procedures ensure that each step in financial handling (receipt, recording, banking, reporting) is not completed by one person?

1082. Has risk management been considered when planning an event?

1083. Does the Firewall Services project team have experience with the technology to be implemented?

1084. Is the auditor able to evaluate contradictory evidence in an unbiased manner?

1085. Are procedures in place to ensure the security of staff and information and compliance with privacy legislation if applicable?

1086. Do you have proper induction processes for all new paid staff and volunteers who have a specific role and responsibility?

1087. Is all required equipment available?

1088. Who audits the auditor?

1089. Have all possible risks/hazards been identified (including injury to staff, damage to equipment, impact on others in the community)?

1090. To what extent should analytical procedures be utilized in the risk-assessment process?

1091. Have reasonable steps been taken to reduce the risks to acceptable levels?

1092. Have top software and customer managers formally committed to support the Firewall Services project?

1093. Are staff committed for the duration of the product?

1094. When your organization is entering into a major contract, does it seek legal advice?

4.5 Contractor Status Report: Firewall Services

1095. Are there contractual transfer concerns?

1096. If applicable; describe your standard schedule for new software version releases. Are new software version releases included in the standard maintenance plan?

1097. What was the final actual cost?

1098. What was the budget or estimated cost for your organizations services?

1099. What process manages the contracts?

1100. What was the overall budget or estimated cost?

1101. What was the actual budget or estimated cost for your organizations services?

1102. How does the proposed individual meet each requirement?

1103. What is the average response time for answering a support call?

1104. How long have you been using the services?

1105. Describe how often regular updates are made to the proposed solution. Are corresponding regular updates included in the standard maintenance plan?

1106. Who can list a Firewall Services project as organization experience, your organization or a previous employee of your organization?

1107. How is risk transferred?

1108. What are the minimum and optimal bandwidth requirements for the proposed solution?

4.6 Formal Acceptance: Firewall Services

1109. What are the requirements against which to test, Who will execute?

1110. What features, practices, and processes proved to be strengths or weaknesses?

1111. Who supplies data?

1112. General estimate of the costs and times to complete the Firewall Services project?

1113. Does it do what client said it would?

1114. Did the Firewall Services project manager and team act in a professional and ethical manner?

1115. Do you buy-in installation services?

1116. What function(s) does it fill or meet?

1117. Was business value realized?

1118. What was done right?

1119. Was the Firewall Services project managed well?

1120. What lessons were learned about your Firewall Services project management methodology?

1121. Was the sponsor/customer satisfied?

1122. Was the Firewall Services project work done on time, within budget, and according to specification?

1123. Did the Firewall Services project achieve its MOV?

1124. Does it do what Firewall Services project team said it would?

1125. What can you do better next time?

1126. How does your team plan to obtain formal acceptance on your Firewall Services project?

1127. What is the Acceptance Management Process?

1128. Was the Firewall Services project goal achieved?

5.0 Closing Process Group: Firewall Services

1129. What will you do?

1130. Can the lesson learned be replicated?

1131. Were risks identified and mitigated?

1132. What was learned?

1133. Did the Firewall Services project management methodology work?

1134. Is the Firewall Services project funded?

1135. Will the Firewall Services project deliverable(s) replace a current asset or group of assets?

1136. Did you do things well?

1137. Are there funding or time constraints?

1138. Were the outcomes different from the already stated planned?

1139. What were things that you did very well and want to do the same again on the next Firewall Services project?

1140. How critical is the Firewall Services project success to the success of your organization?

1141. Who are the Firewall Services project stakeholders?

1142. What is the risk of failure to your organization?

1143. What do you need to do?

1144. What can you do better next time, and what specific actions can you take to improve?

5.1 Procurement Audit: Firewall Services

1145. Was there reasonable justification for the need of the purchase, namely when made towards the end of the financial year?

1146. Where required, did candidates give evidence of complying with quality assurance standards?

1147. Is the functioning of automatic disbursement programs tested by an independent party?

1148. Does the strategy ensure that the best supplier is chosen considering: price, quality, service, dependable operation, internal operation costs, life time operation costs and codes of ethic?

1149. Are travel expenditures monitored to determine that they are in line with other employees and reasonable for the area of travel?

1150. Is there a formal program of inservice training for personnel in the business management function?

1151. Are approval limits covered in written procedures?

1152. Were all interested operators allowed the opportunity to participate?

1153. Are the official minutes written in a clear and concise manner?

1154. Do contracts contain regular reviews, targets and quality standards in order to assess suppliers performance?

1155. Are goods generally ordered and received in time to be used in the programs for which they were ordered?

1156. Is it tested periodically, whether your organizations way of handling tasks is competitive in relation to price and quality?

1157. Were no tenders presented after the time limit accepted?

1158. Does your organization use existing contracts where possible to avoid the cost of bidding?

1159. Are existing suppliers that have a special right to be consulted being contacted?

1160. Are there regular accounting reconciliations of contract payments, transactions and inventory?

1161. Is procurement execution duly monitored and documented?

1162. Is the procurement process well organized?

1163. Is there ineffective internal communication in the procurement function/unit?

1164. Are there procedures governing how sales and use tax will be handled (ordering in state versus ordering out of state)?

5.2 Contract Close-Out: Firewall Services

1165. How does it work?

1166. Parties: Authorized?

1167. Have all contracts been completed?

1168. Why Outsource?

1169. Change in knowledge?

1170. What happens to the recipient of services?

1171. Has each contract been audited to verify acceptance and delivery?

1172. Are the signers the authorized officials?

1173. Was the contract type appropriate?

1174. Was the contract sufficiently clear so as not to result in numerous disputes and misunderstandings?

1175. Have all acceptance criteria been met prior to final payment to contractors?

1176. How/when used ?

1177. How is the contracting office notified of the automatic contract close-out?

1178. Change in circumstances?

1179. Have all contracts been closed?

1180. Was the contract complete without requiring numerous changes and revisions?

1181. What is capture management?

1182. Have all contract records been included in the Firewall Services project archives?

1183. Change in attitude or behavior?

1184. Parties: who is involved?

5.3 Project or Phase Close-Out: Firewall Services

1185. Was the schedule met?

1186. What security considerations needed to be addressed during the procurement life cycle?

1187. What are they?

1188. Have business partners been involved extensively, and what data was required for them?

1189. What could be done to improve the process?

1190. If you were the Firewall Services project sponsor, how would you determine which Firewall Services project team(s) and/or individuals deserve recognition?

1191. Who is responsible for award close-out?

1192. What stakeholder group needs, expectations, and interests are being met by the Firewall Services project?

1193. What information did each stakeholder need to contribute to the Firewall Services projects success?

1194. What was expected from each stakeholder?

1195. Which changes might a stakeholder be required to make as a result of the Firewall Services project?

1196. What information is each stakeholder group interested in?

1197. Who controlled the resources for the Firewall Services project?

1198. How often did each stakeholder need an update?

1199. What were the goals and objectives of the communications strategy for the Firewall Services project?

1200. What was the preferred delivery mechanism?

1201. What benefits or impacts does the stakeholder group expect to obtain as a result of the Firewall Services project?

1202. Who exerted influence that has positively affected or negatively impacted the Firewall Services project?

5.4 Lessons Learned: Firewall Services

1203. Were cost budgets met?

1204. Were the Firewall Services project objectives met (if not, briefly account for what wasnt met)?

1205. How well do you feel the executives supported this Firewall Services project?

1206. How objective was the collection of data?

1207. For the next Firewall Services project, how could you improve on the way Firewall Services project was conducted?

1208. What were the key issues?

1209. How useful do individuals find communications?

1210. Will the information remain current?

1211. What was helpful to know when planning the deployment?

1212. How much time is required for the task?

1213. What is the impact of tax policy on the case?

1214. What things mattered the most on this Firewall Services project?

1215. How effective were Firewall Services project

audits?

1216. How effective was each Firewall Services project Team member in fulfilling his/her role?

1217. How effective were Best Practices & Lessons Learned from prior Firewall Services projects utilized in this Firewall Services project?

1218. What was the single greatest success and the single greatest shortcoming or challenge from the Firewall Services projects perspective?

1219. What would you approach differently next time?

1220. How effectively were issues managed on the Firewall Services project?

1221. Is your organization willing to expose problems or mistakes for the betterment of the collective whole, and can you do this in a way that does not intimidate employees or workers?

1222. What is the supplier dependency?

Index

collect 67, 95, 177, 181, 230
collected   32, 36, 62, 65, 67-68, 180
collection   61, 184, 257
collective   223, 258
combine   84
coming   61, 207
command   92
comments   207
commit   172, 205
commitment   90, 105
committed   62, 138, 148, 243-244
committee   137, 180, 204
common   174, 233
community   168, 176-177, 202, 244
companies   1, 99, 167, 221
company   7, 51, 68, 103, 107, 109, 116-118
comparable   136
compare   57, 80, 241
compared   105, 154, 179
comparing   136
comparison   10, 240
compatible   218, 238
compelling   28
competing   46
competitor   131, 239
complain   180, 182
complaint   222
complaints   196
complete   1, 8, 10, 24, 31, 34, 135, 146, 155, 158-159, 164,
166, 169, 200, 227, 247, 254
completed   11, 31-32, 34, 40, 146, 162, 190, 195, 225, 243, 253
completely   114, 137, 168
completing   113, 149
completion   30, 32, 151, 161, 174, 179, 186, 238, 242
complex   7, 106, 147, 242
complexity   21, 55, 68, 146
compliance   17, 44, 55, 61, 77, 243
complied   225
complying   251
components   148, 190
compute   11
computing   114
concept   81, 146, 184

reports 51, 94, 130, 172, 175, 204, 222, 240
repository   154
represent   78, 218
reproduced   1
reputation   113
request   5, 67, 179, 216-219
requested   1, 79, 219
requests   207, 216-217
require 36, 52, 60, 64, 92, 163, 237
required   16, 18, 29, 31, 33-34, 39, 47, 71, 78, 82, 87, 97,
127, 139, 155, 157, 171, 182, 184, 188, 210, 244, 251, 255, 257
requiring   130, 254
research   18, 106, 114, 131, 146, 167, 222
reserved   1
reserves   151
reside 81
resistance   211
resolution   68
resolve 16, 21-22, 225, 227
resolved   173, 195, 235
resource   3-4, 102, 140, 148, 163-165, 190, 212, 215
resources   2, 7, 17, 20-21, 28, 41, 46, 63, 78, 96-97, 101-102,
114, 126, 128, 132, 153, 157-158, 164, 168, 170, 176, 205, 233,
237-238, 256
respect   1
respond   196
responded   11
response   18, 21, 90, 92, 95, 97, 207, 245
responses   106, 196
responsive   168, 177
restrict 142
result   60, 75, 78, 176, 178, 182, 211, 219, 253, 255-256
resulted   94, 231
resulting   70, 191
results 8, 35, 38, 57, 73-75, 77, 79-80, 84-85, 87, 91-92, 126-127,
135, 157, 170, 177, 184, 212, 223, 235
retain   100, 180
retained   66
retention   167
retrospect   118
return   75, 113, 184-185
revenue   16, 51
review 9, 39, 60, 128, 173-174, 178, 186, 196, 221, 223, 232

select 67, 95
selected   76, 177
selecting   63, 105, 136
selection   5, 206, 213, 229
sellers 1
selling 116, 159, 221
senior 90, 103-104, 181
sensitive   35
separated   187
sequence   155
sequencing   101, 134, 166, 205
series 10
seriously   132
service 1-2, 7, 53, 73, 77, 82, 97, 106, 160, 178, 207, 214-215, 251
Services   1-13, 15-42, 44-87, 89-96, 98-99, 101-131, 133-143,
145-157, 159, 161-182, 184, 186-188, 190, 192-202, 204-206, 208-
210, 212-220, 222, 225-229, 231, 233, 235, 237, 239-251, 253-258
session 155
setbacks   65-66
setting 115, 121
Several65, 200
severely   63
shared 88, 133, 141, 177, 221
sharing84, 97, 126, 211, 237
sheets 140
shifts 23
short-term   230
should 7, 21-23, 32, 34, 40, 51, 54, 57, 63, 65-67, 70, 81, 89, 96,
106, 110, 112, 120, 122-123, 130, 132-135, 139-140, 145-146, 148,
155-156, 159, 164, 173-174, 184, 188-189, 194-198, 200, 206-207,
219, 225, 244
signature   123
signatures   163
signers 253
similar 35, 40, 57, 63, 80, 157-158, 175, 182, 193, 199-200
simple 106, 242
simply 8, 221
single 107, 239, 258
single-use   7
situation   19, 43, 127, 197, 201, 213, 241
skeptical   111
skills 19, 23, 68, 102, 115, 120, 126, 166, 187-188, 190-191, 204,
229, 238